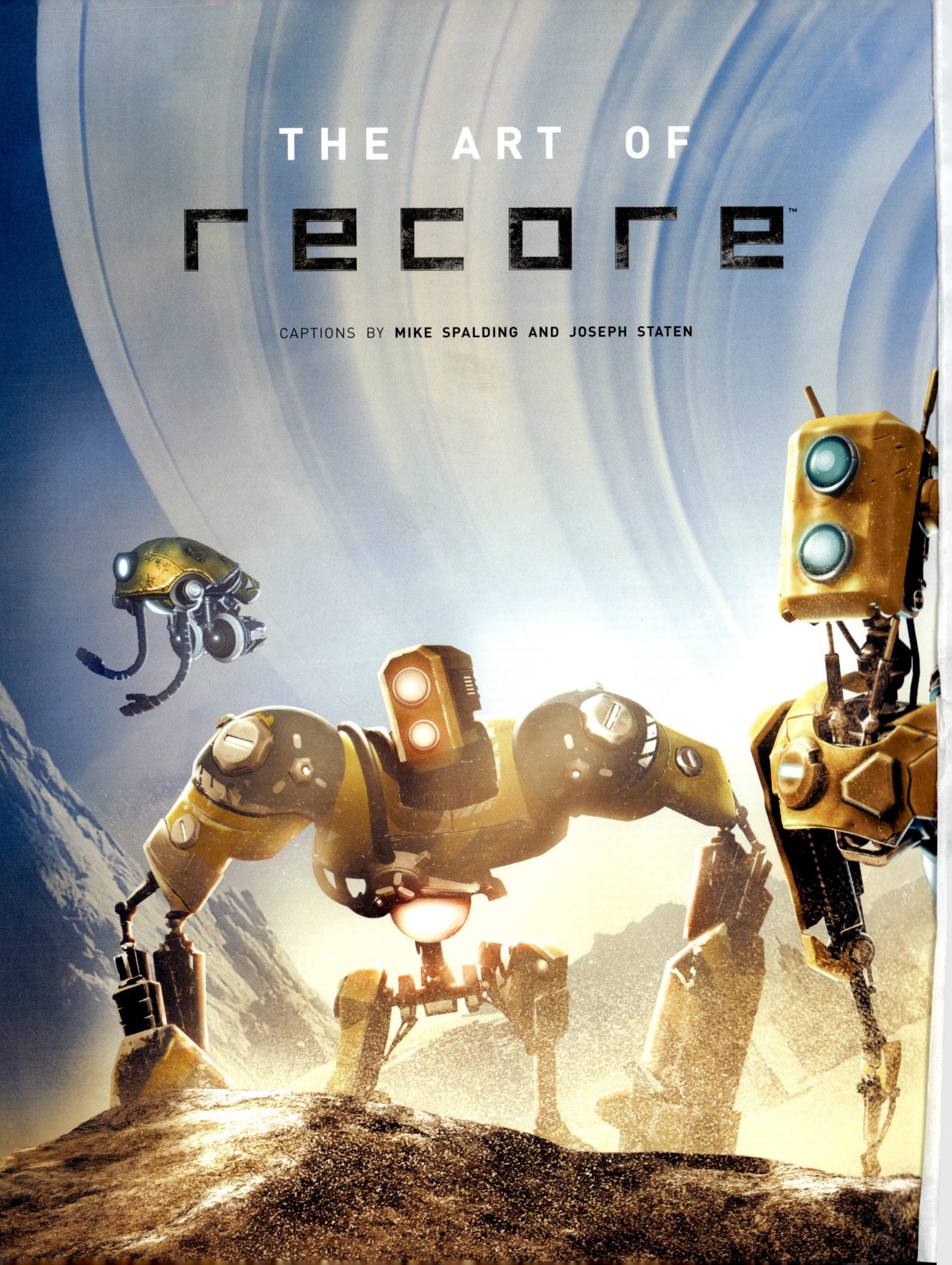

THE ART OF recore™

CAPTIONS BY **MIKE SPALDING AND JOSEPH STATEN**

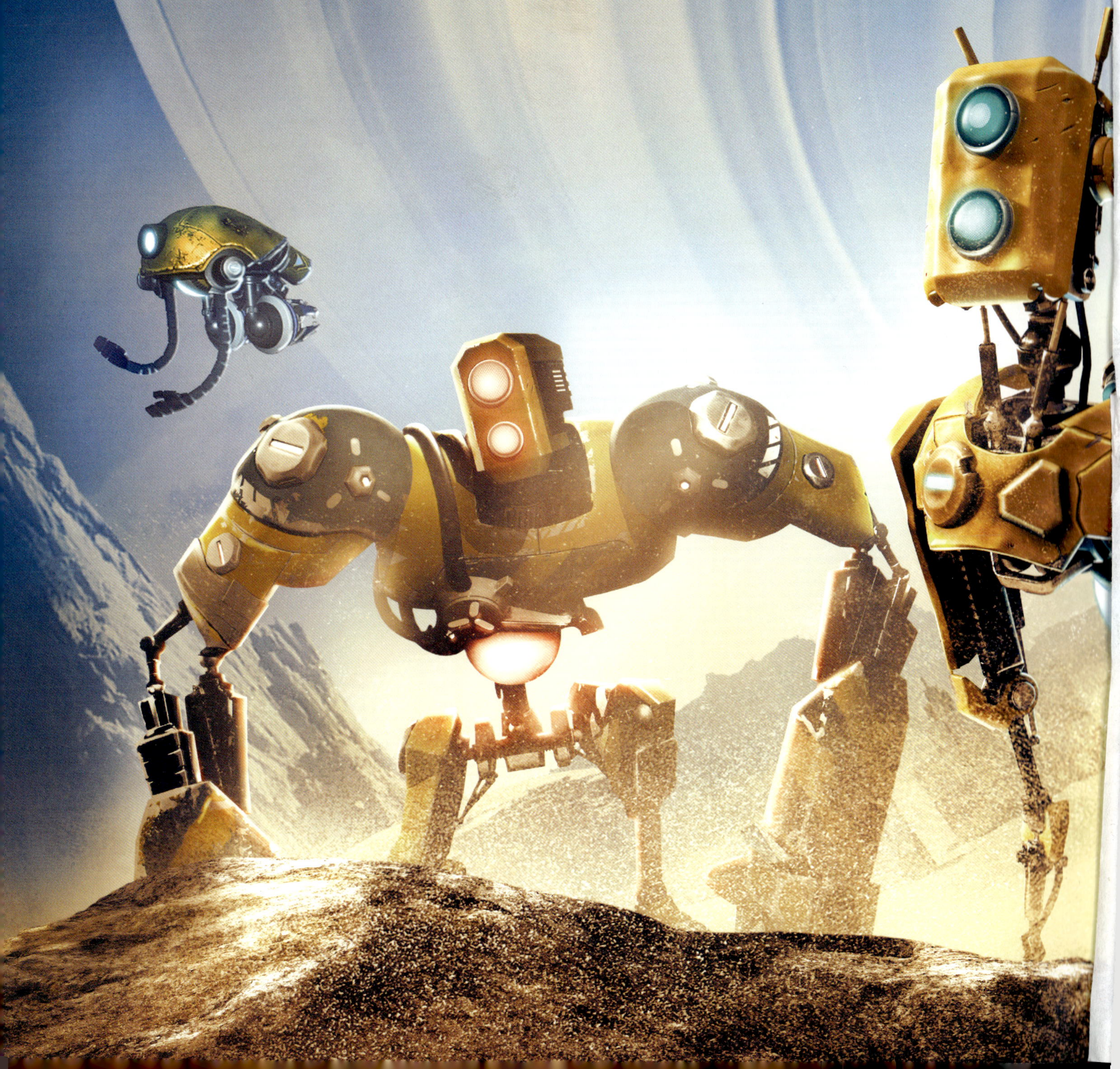

THE ART OF

recore™

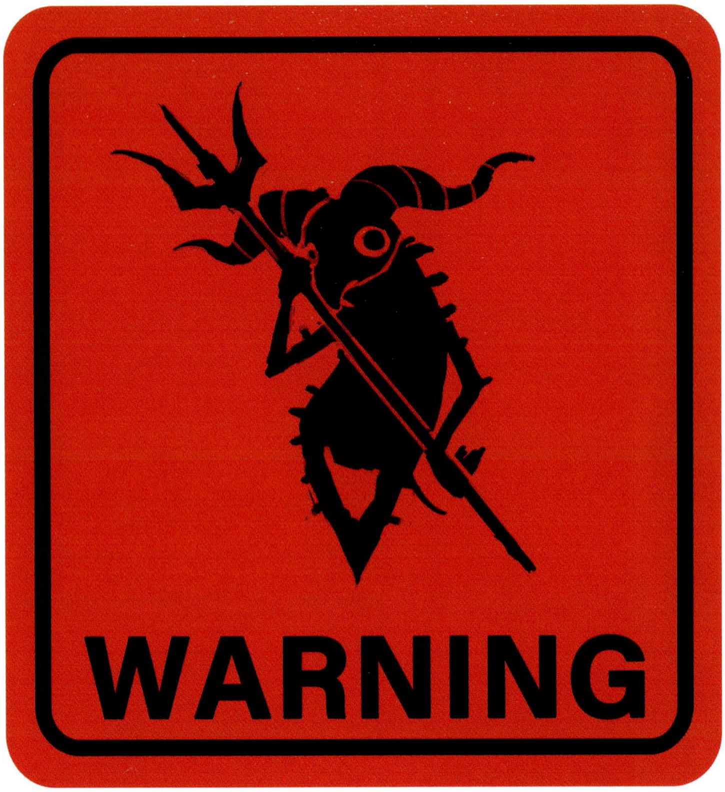
WARNING

Daiki Kasubuchi

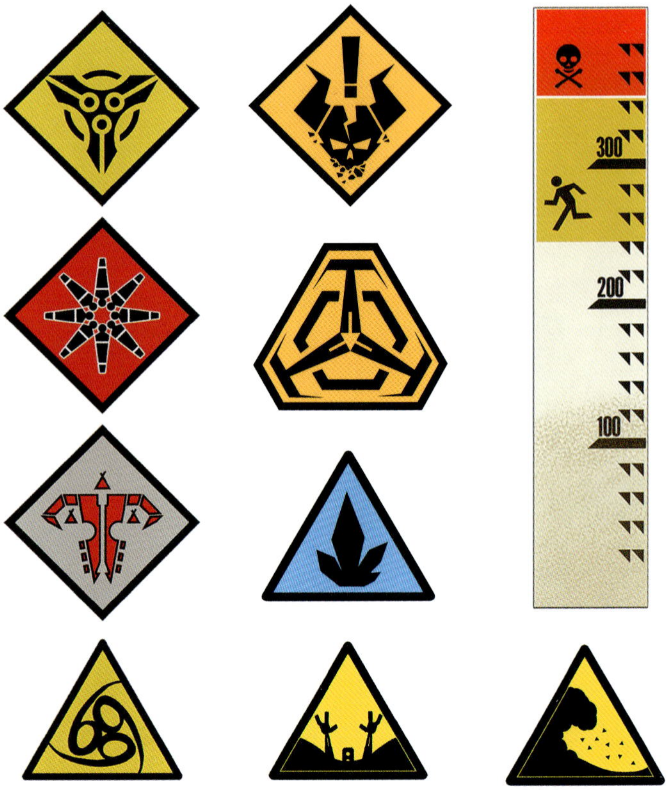
300
200
100

Patrick Shettlesworth

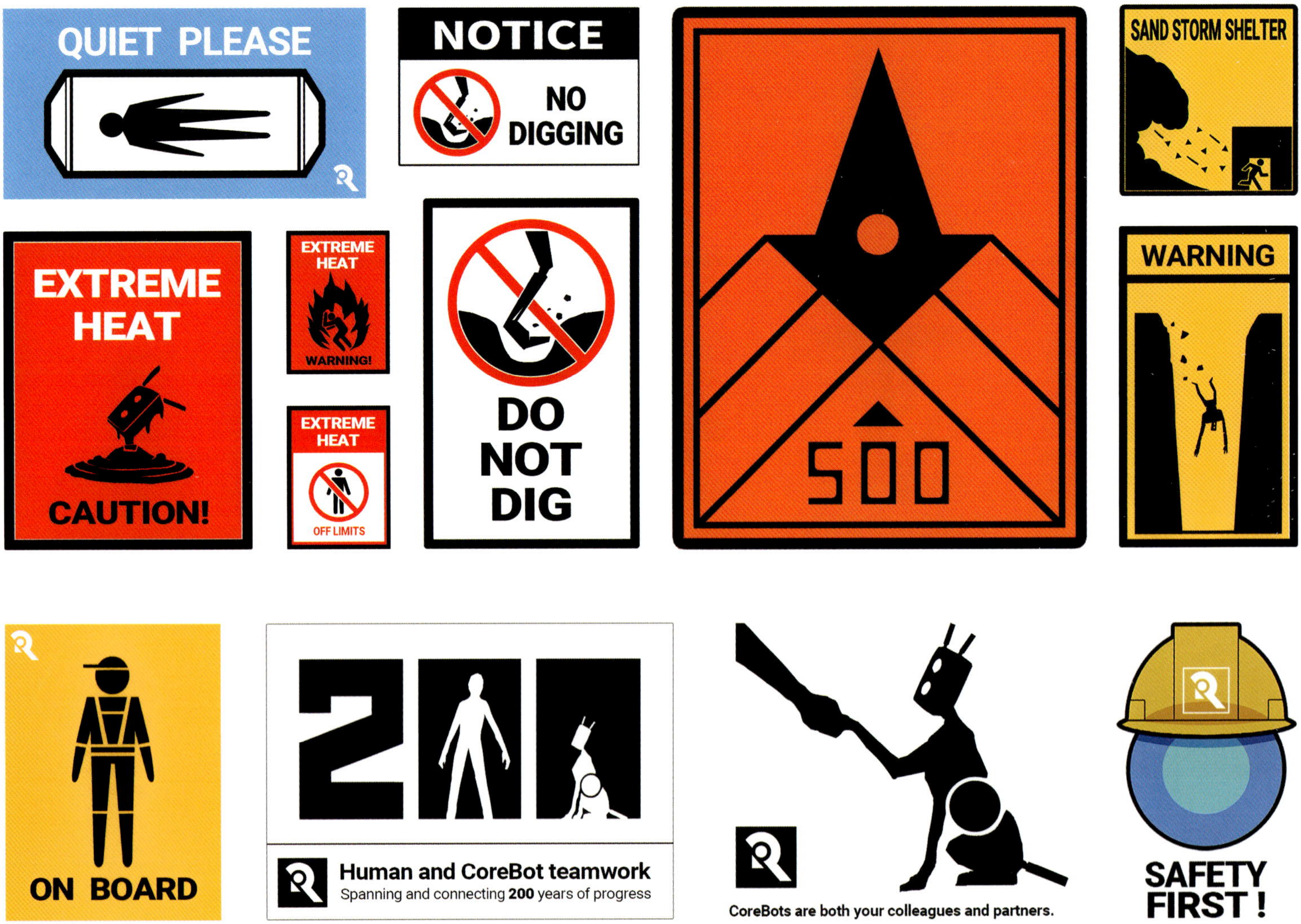
QUIET PLEASE
NOTICE
NO DIGGING
SAND STORM SHELTER
EXTREME HEAT
CAUTION!
EXTREME HEAT
WARNING!
EXTREME HEAT
OFF LIMITS
DO NOT DIG
500
WARNING
ON BOARD
200
Human and CoreBot teamwork
Spanning and connecting 200 years of progress
CoreBots are both your colleagues and partners.
SAFETY FIRST !

Daiki Kasubuchi

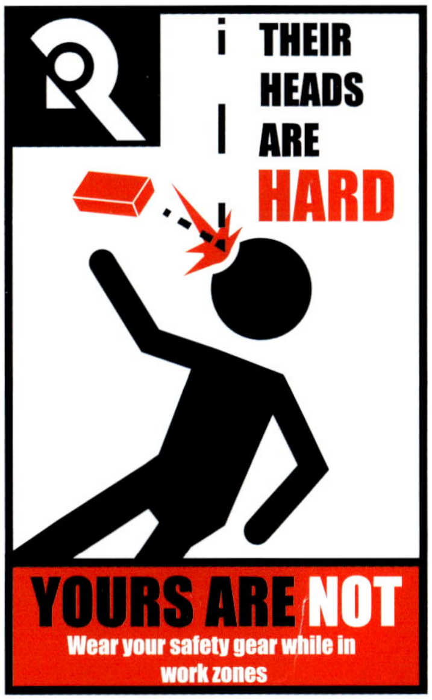
THEIR
HEADS
ARE
HARD
YOURS ARE NOT
Wear your safety gear while in work zones

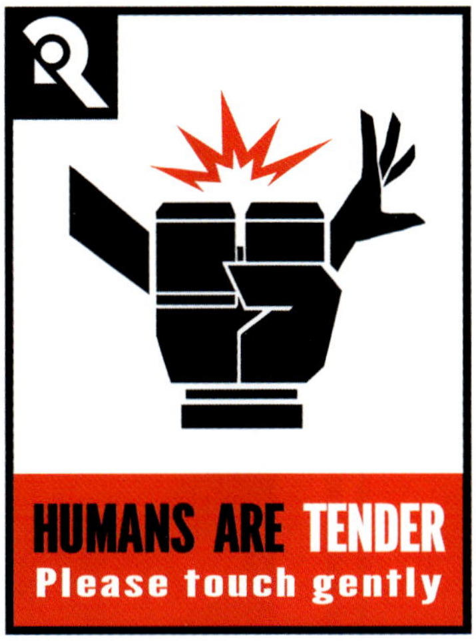
HUMANS ARE TENDER
Please touch gently

Daiki Kasubuchi

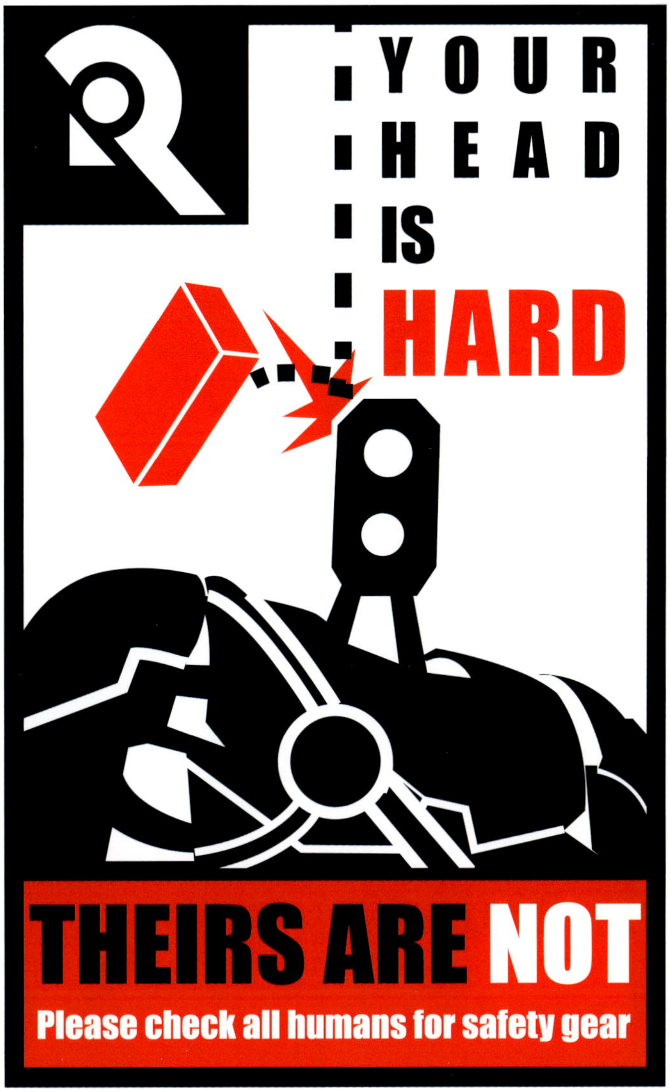
YOUR
HEAD
IS
HARD
THEIRS ARE NOT
Please check all humans for safety gear

Patrick Shettlesworth

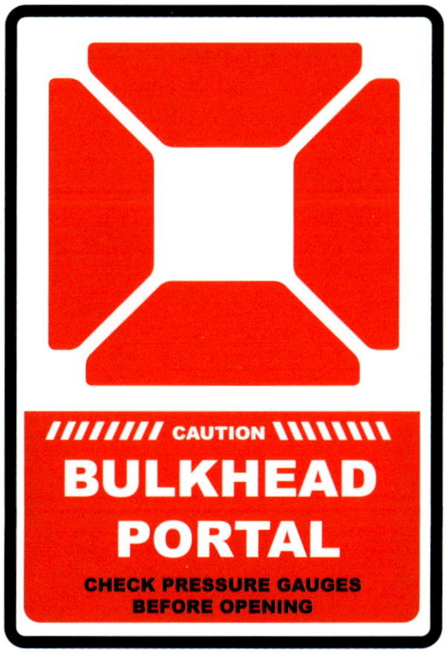
CAUTION
BULKHEAD
PORTAL
CHECK PRESSURE GAUGES
BEFORE OPENING

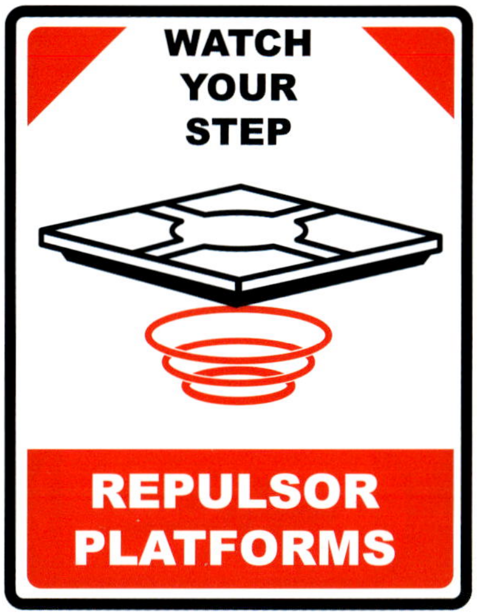
WATCH
YOUR
STEP
REPULSOR
PLATFORMS

Patrick Shettlesworth

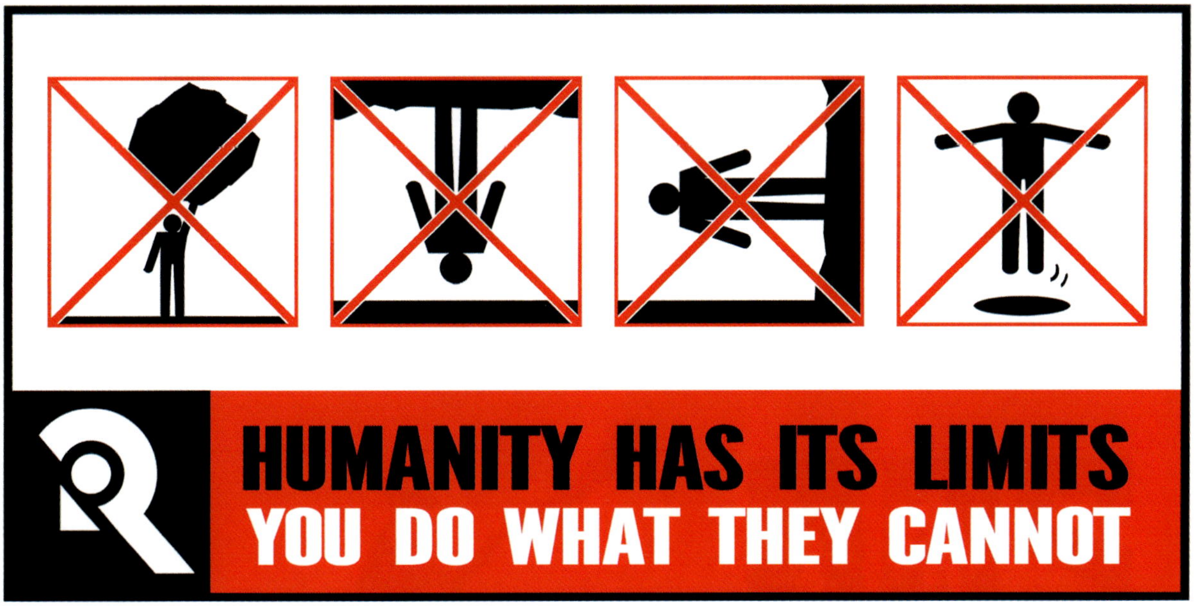
HUMANITY HAS ITS LIMITS
YOU DO WHAT THEY CANNOT

Daiki Kasubuchi

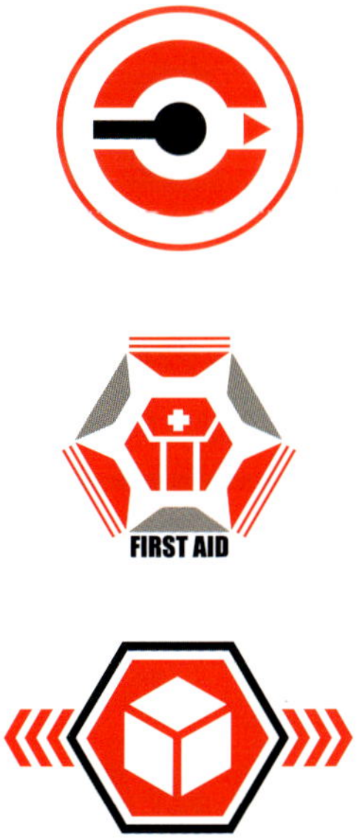
FIRST AID

Patrick Shettlesworth

Safety posters in Far Eden facilities were designed for human and Corebot workers. On the facing page are propaganda posters from the Corebot revolutionary war. These images include alphanumeric shapes from the Corebot symbolic language known as "Digimote."

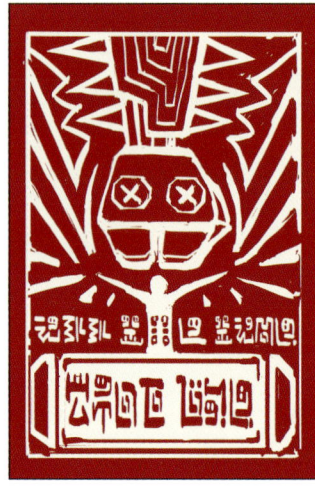
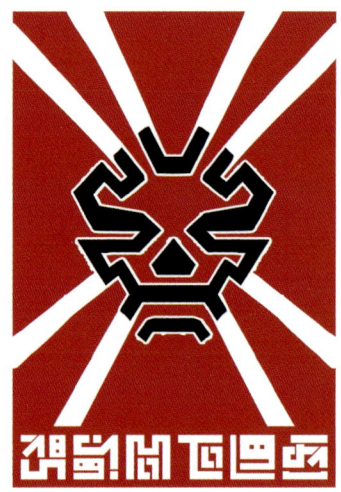
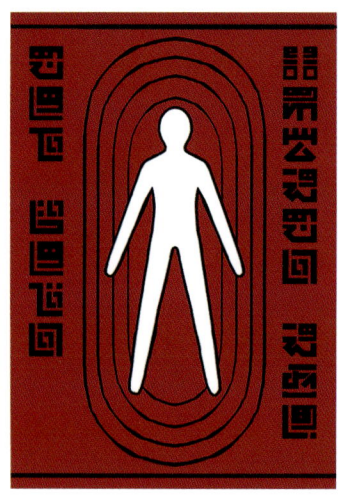
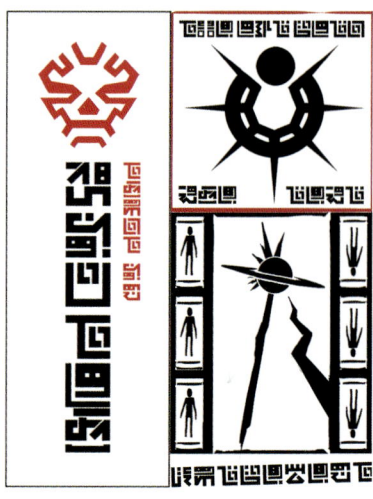
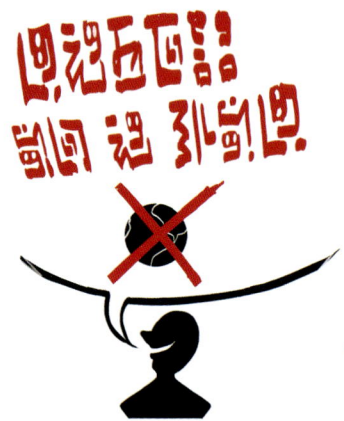
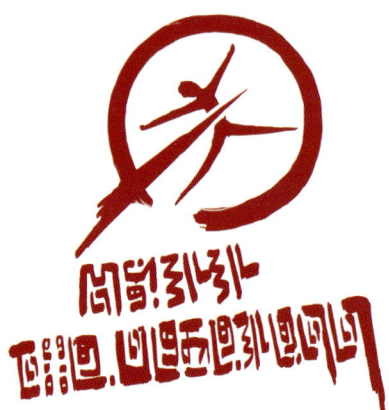
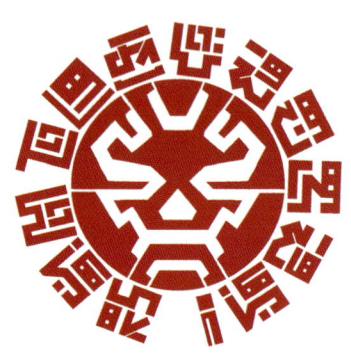
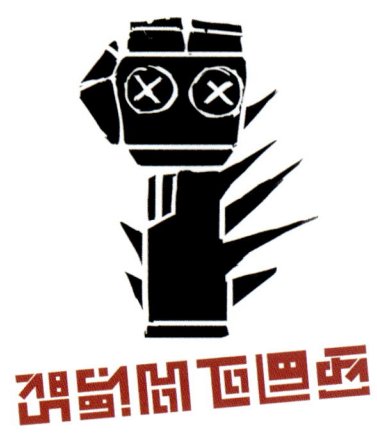
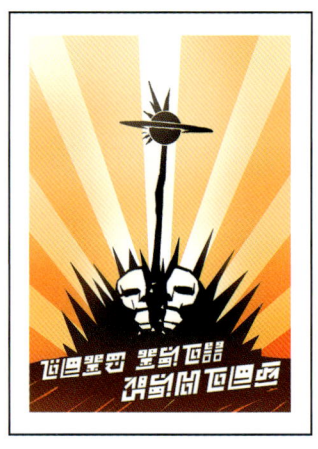
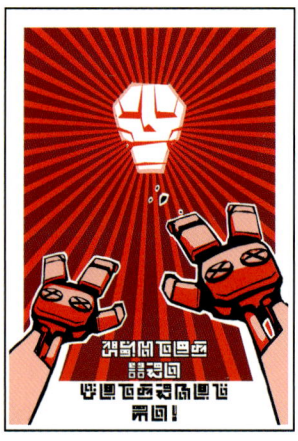
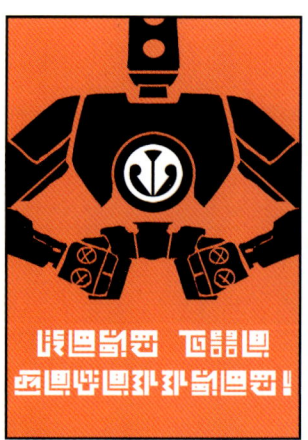
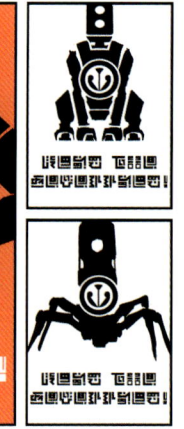
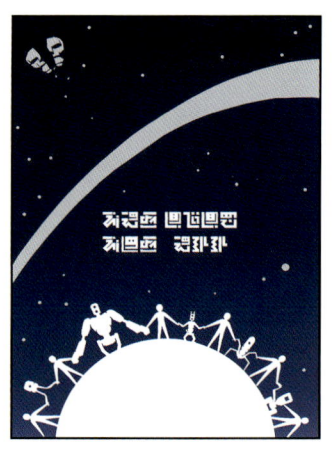
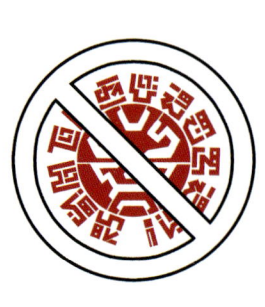
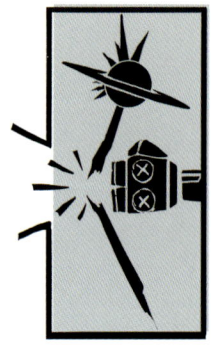
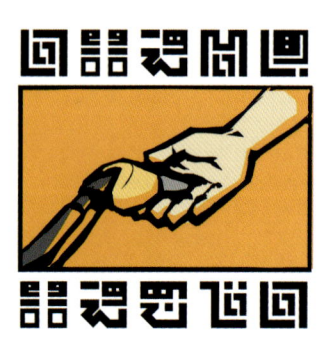
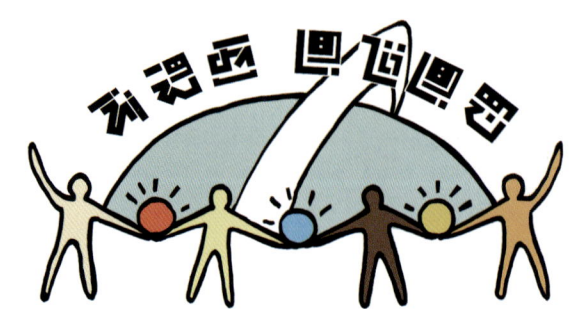

Daiki Kasubuchi

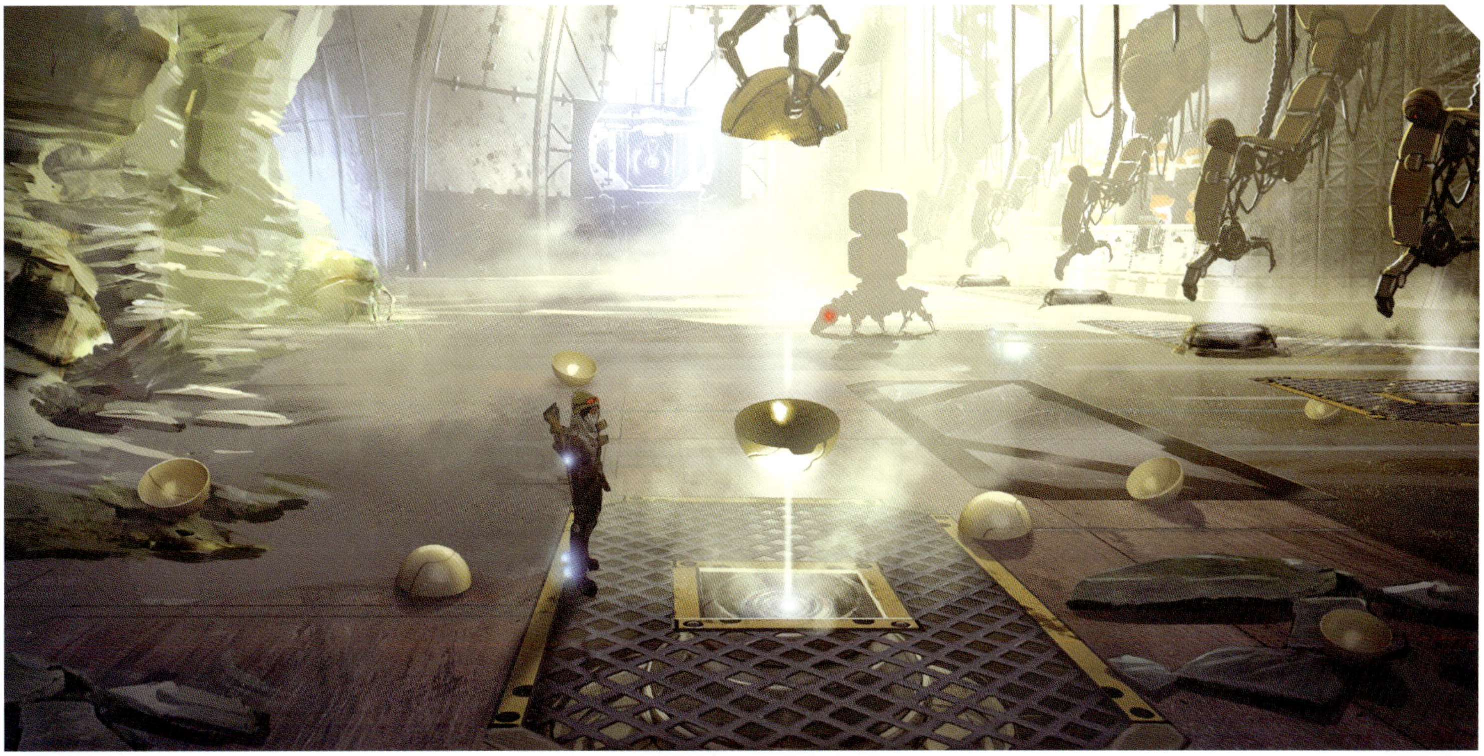

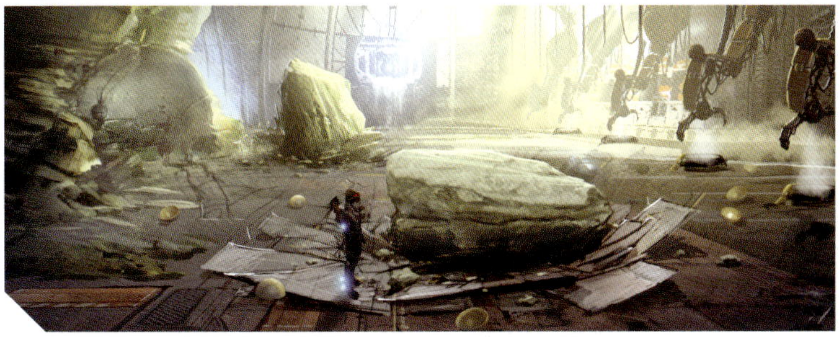

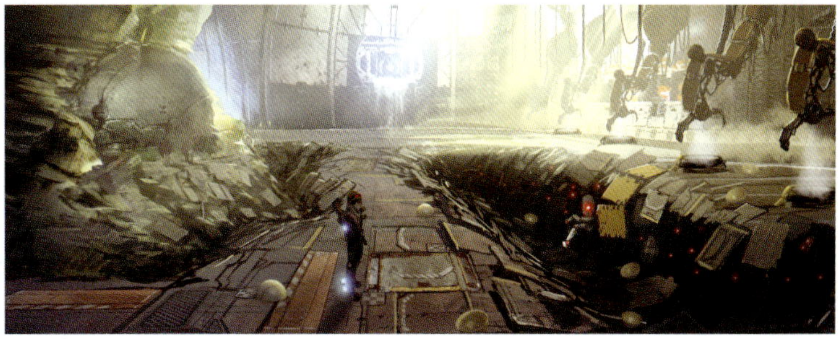

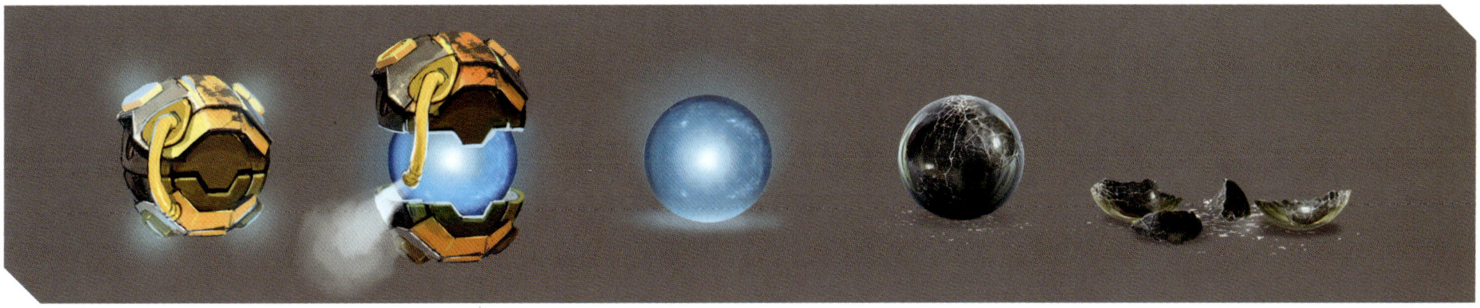

Damien Papet

THE CORE FOUNDRY

Colored in greens and yellows, the Core Foundry is a giant facility filled with Corebot technology that has been mysteriously abandoned. As the player journeys farther into the depths of the foundry, we wanted it to feel progressively more hostile to humans. Signage would be defaced with Digimote graffiti sympathetic to Victor, the platforming would grow more dangerous, and the machinery would take on aggressive forms.

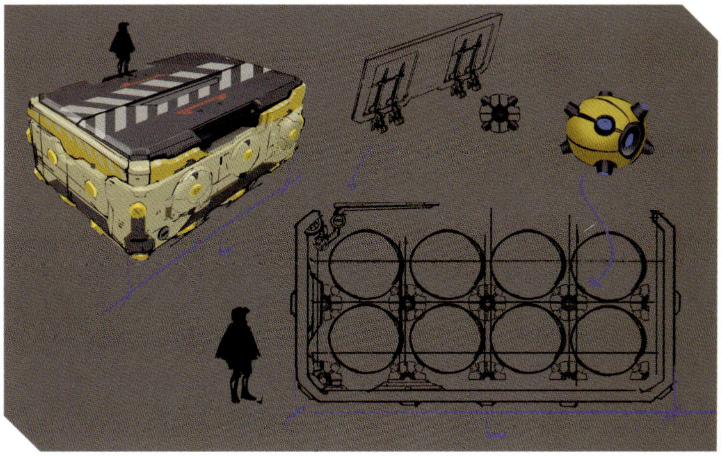

Antoine Lysson

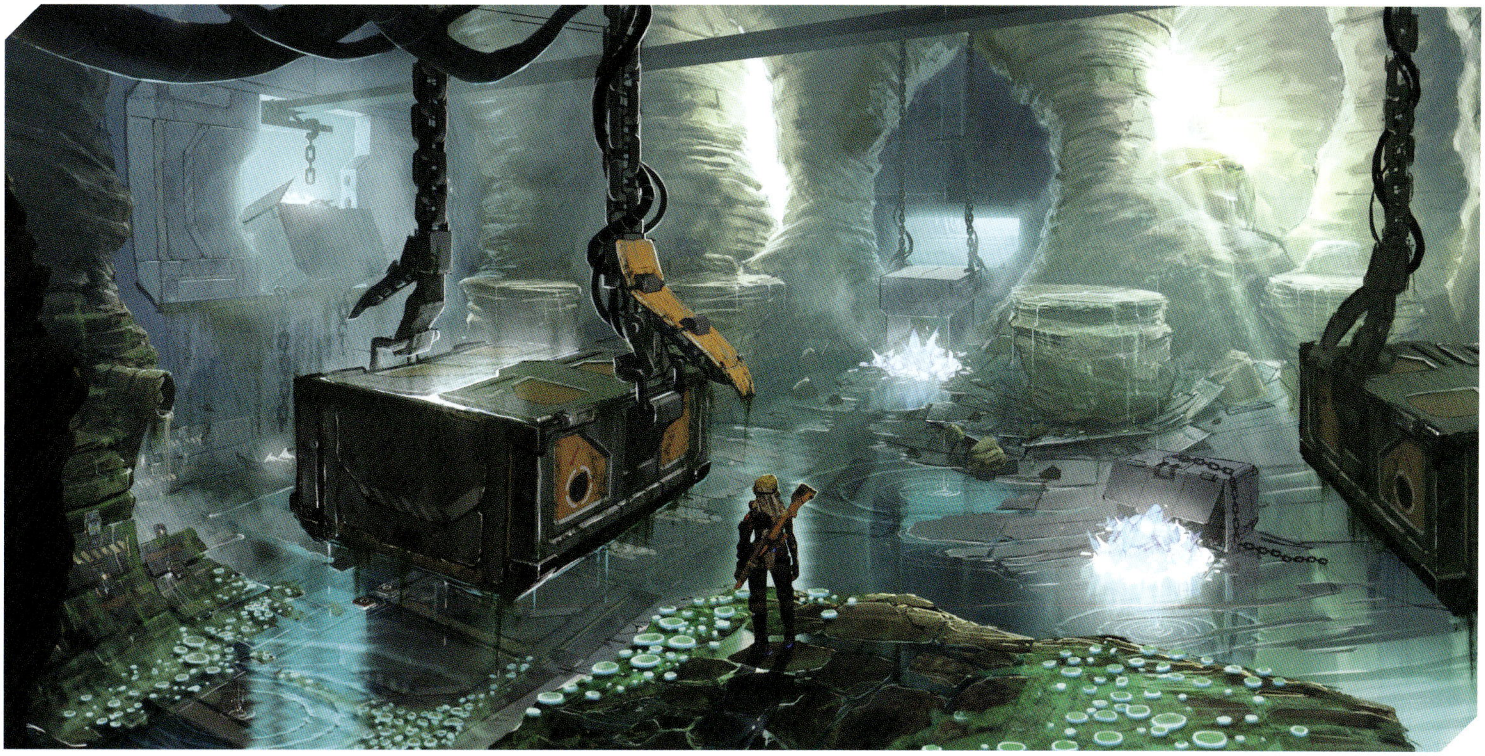

Damien Papet

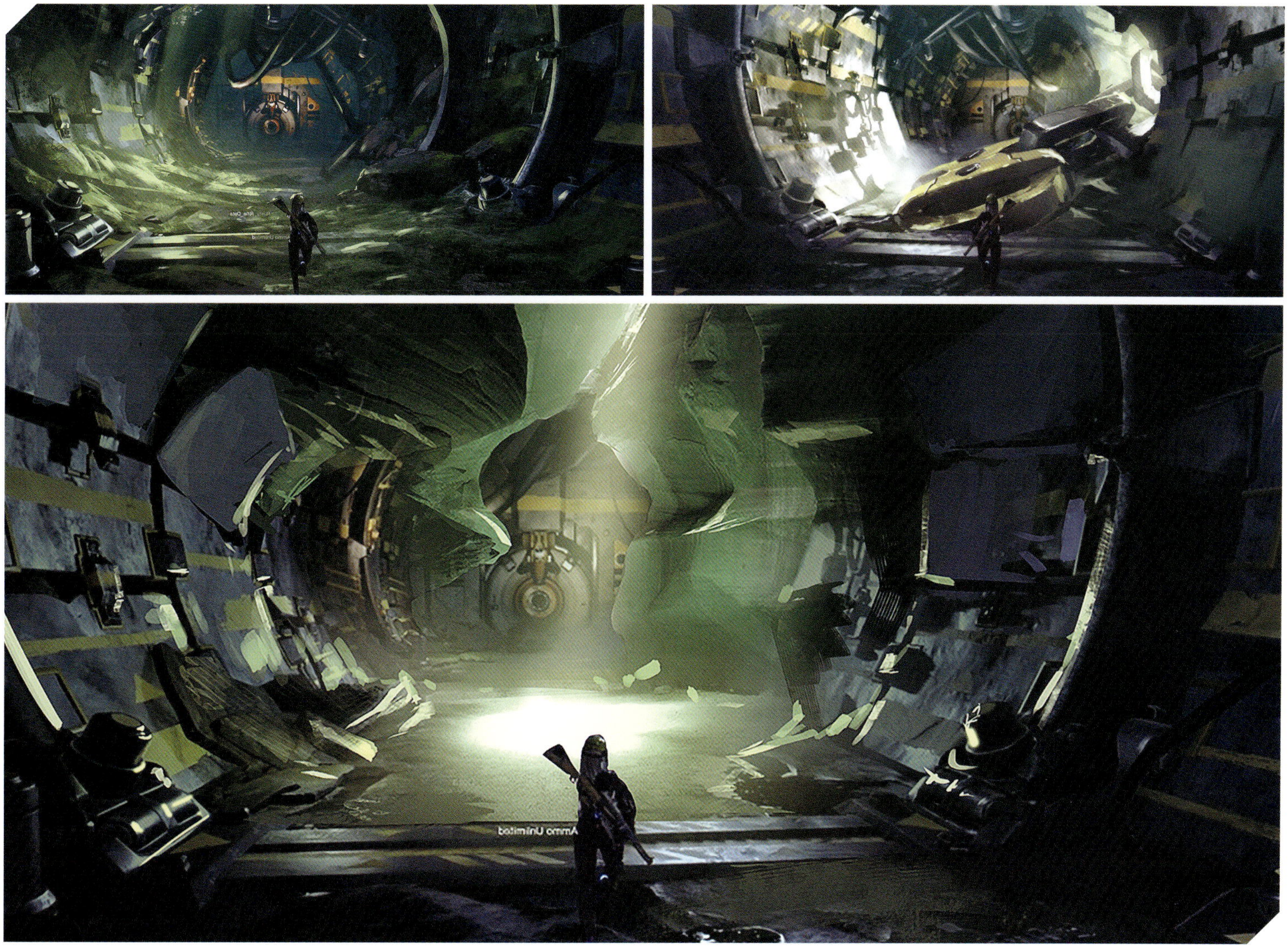

Antoine Lysson

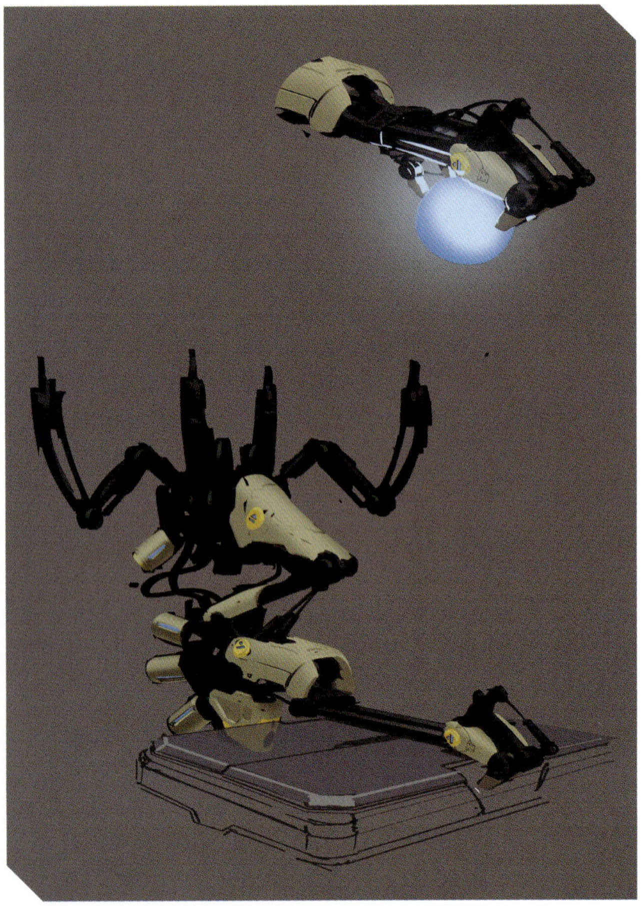

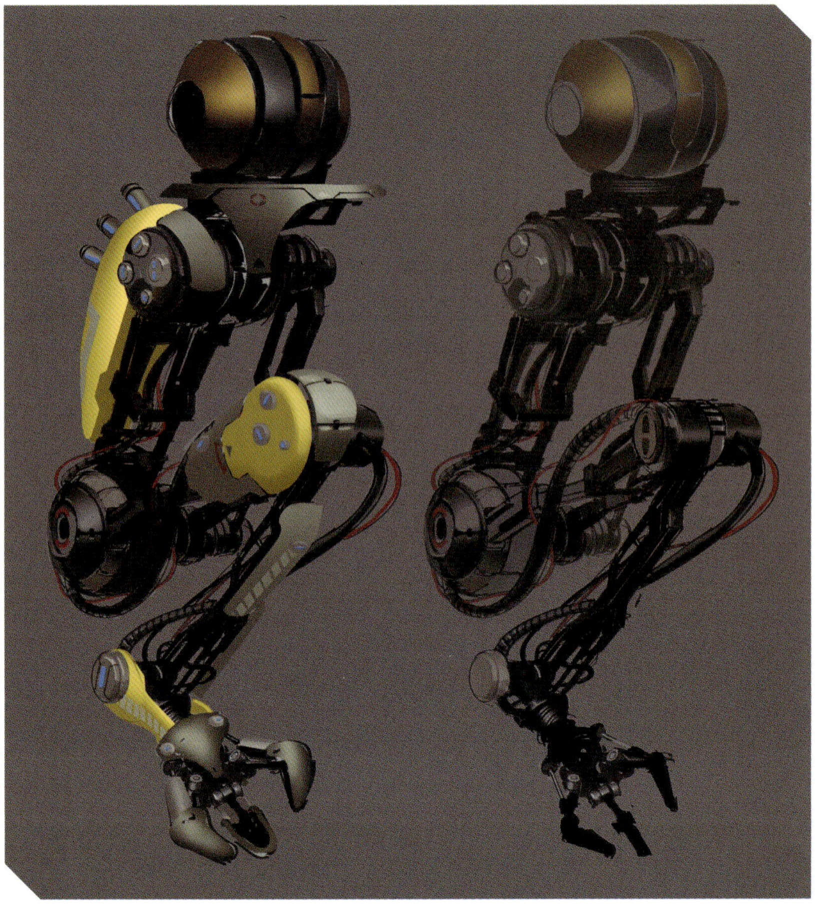

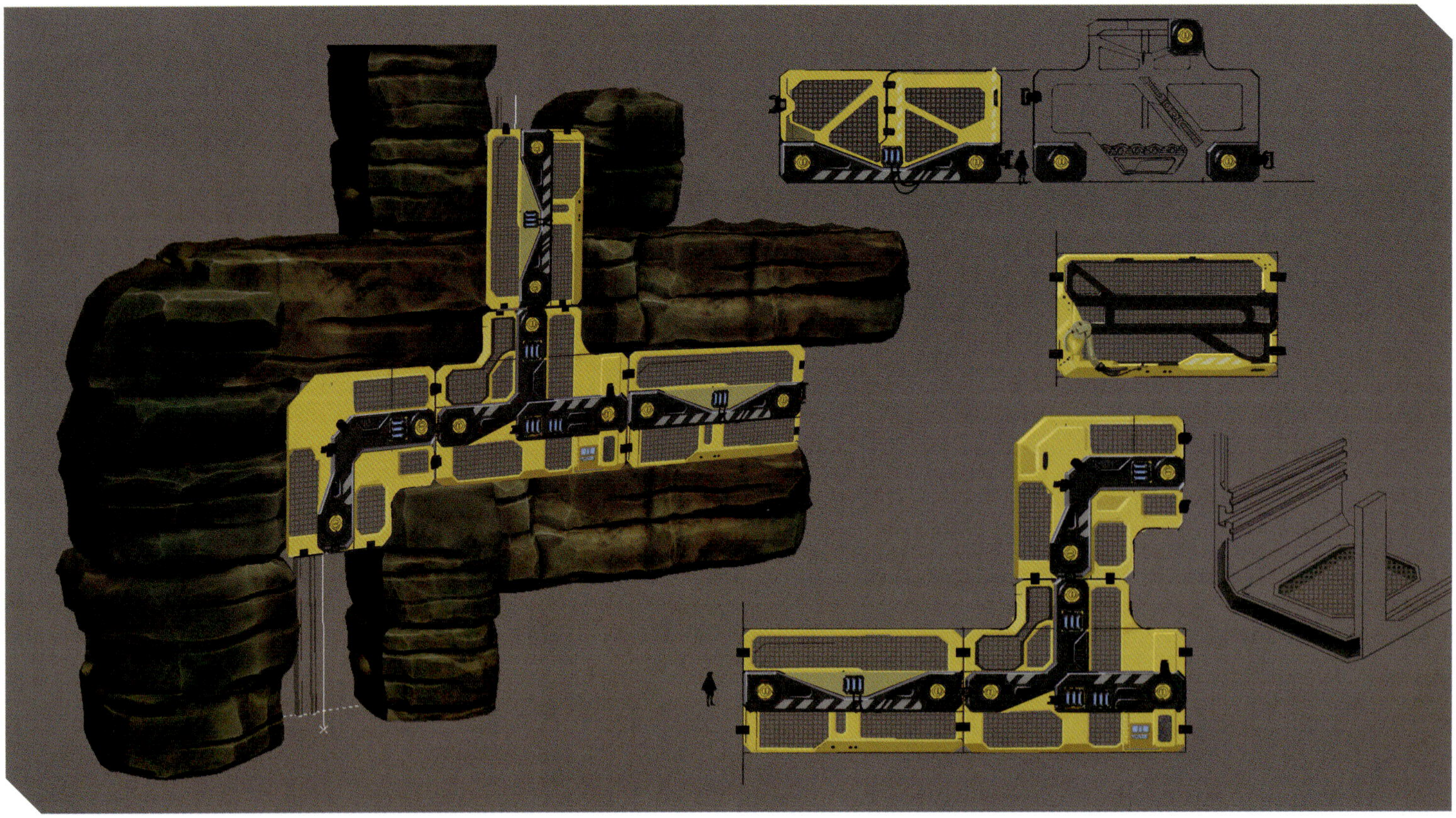

Antoine Lysson

The foundry machinery was designed using the same guidelines as the Corebots—large, yellow, geometric metal shapes over black metal skeletons. These mechanical elements also helped the player find interactive elements, such as the Spider Rails seen above.

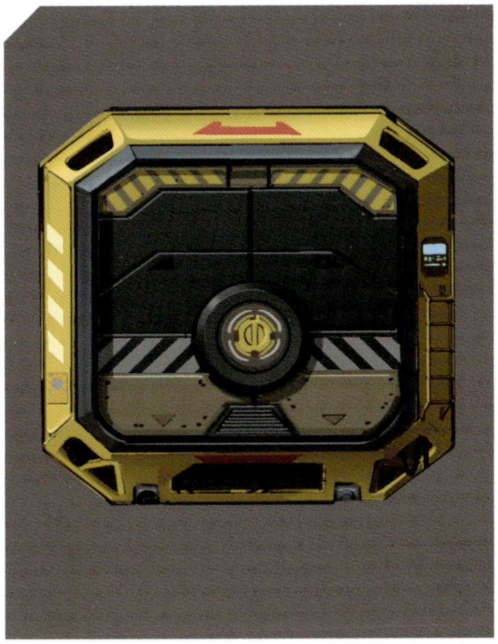

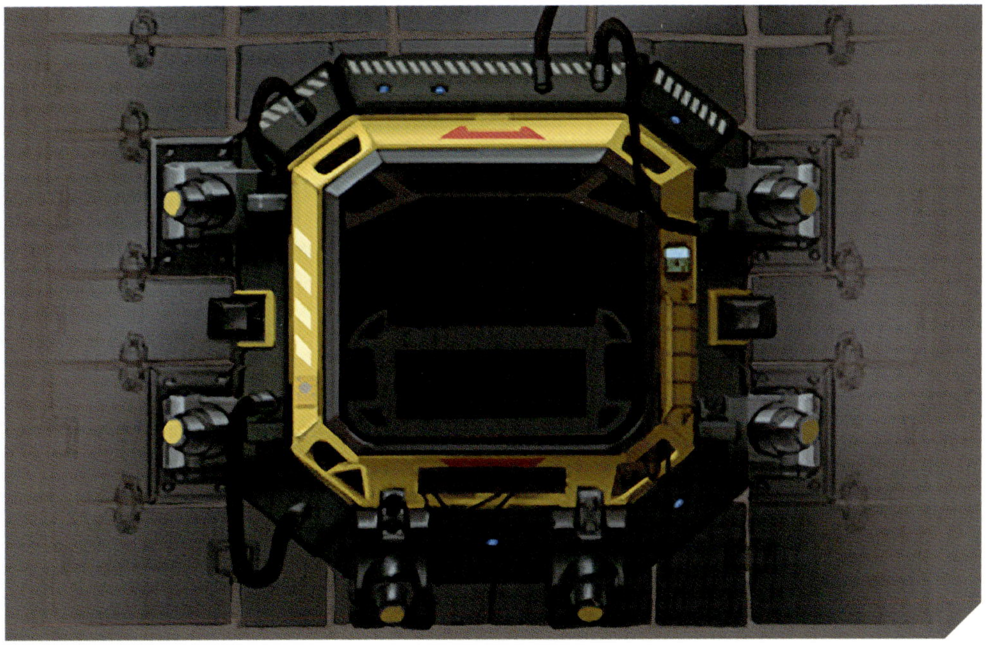

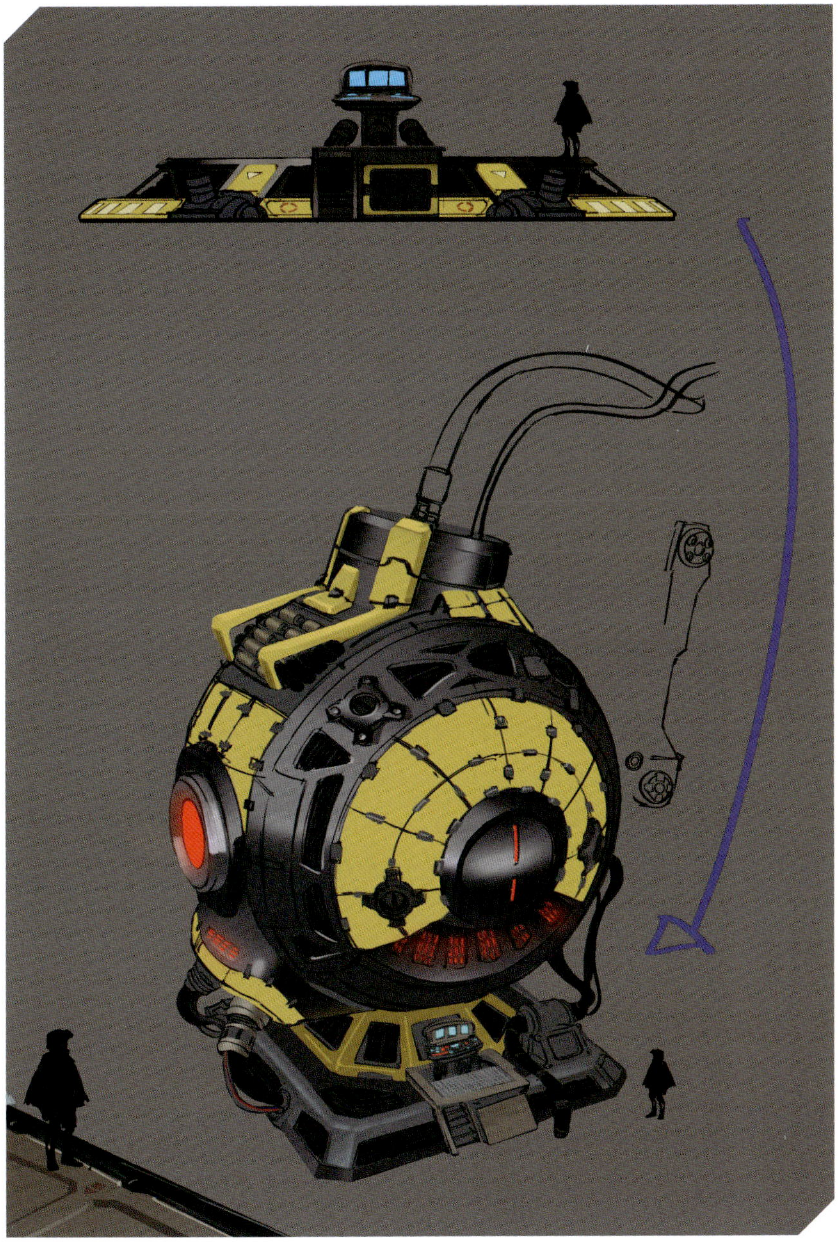

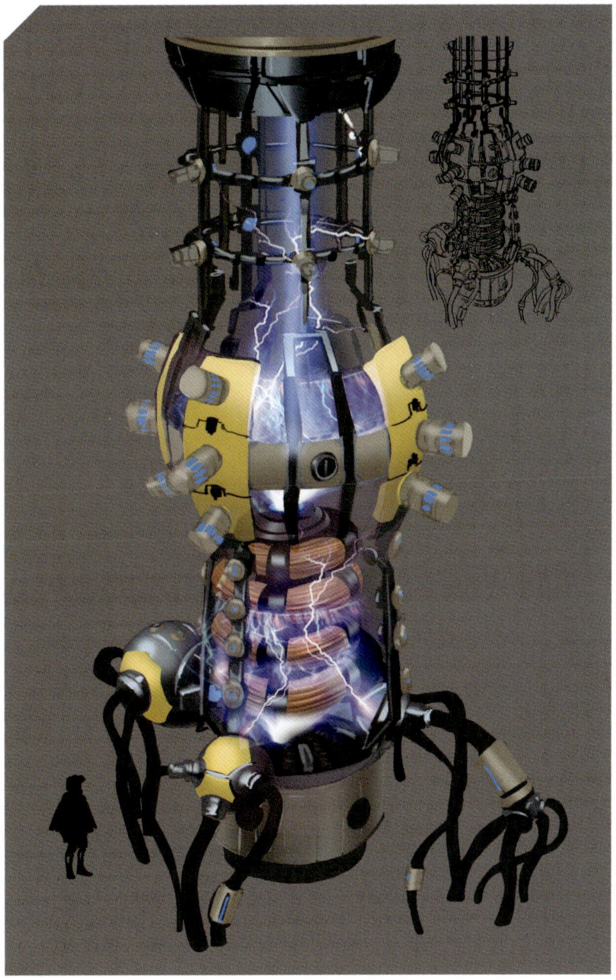

The scale of the machinery was used to show how foreign the world of the Corebots was to humans. With this in mind, we needed to make sure there were enough human-sized elements on the machines to make them seem large, rather than making Joule seem small.

Antoine Lysson

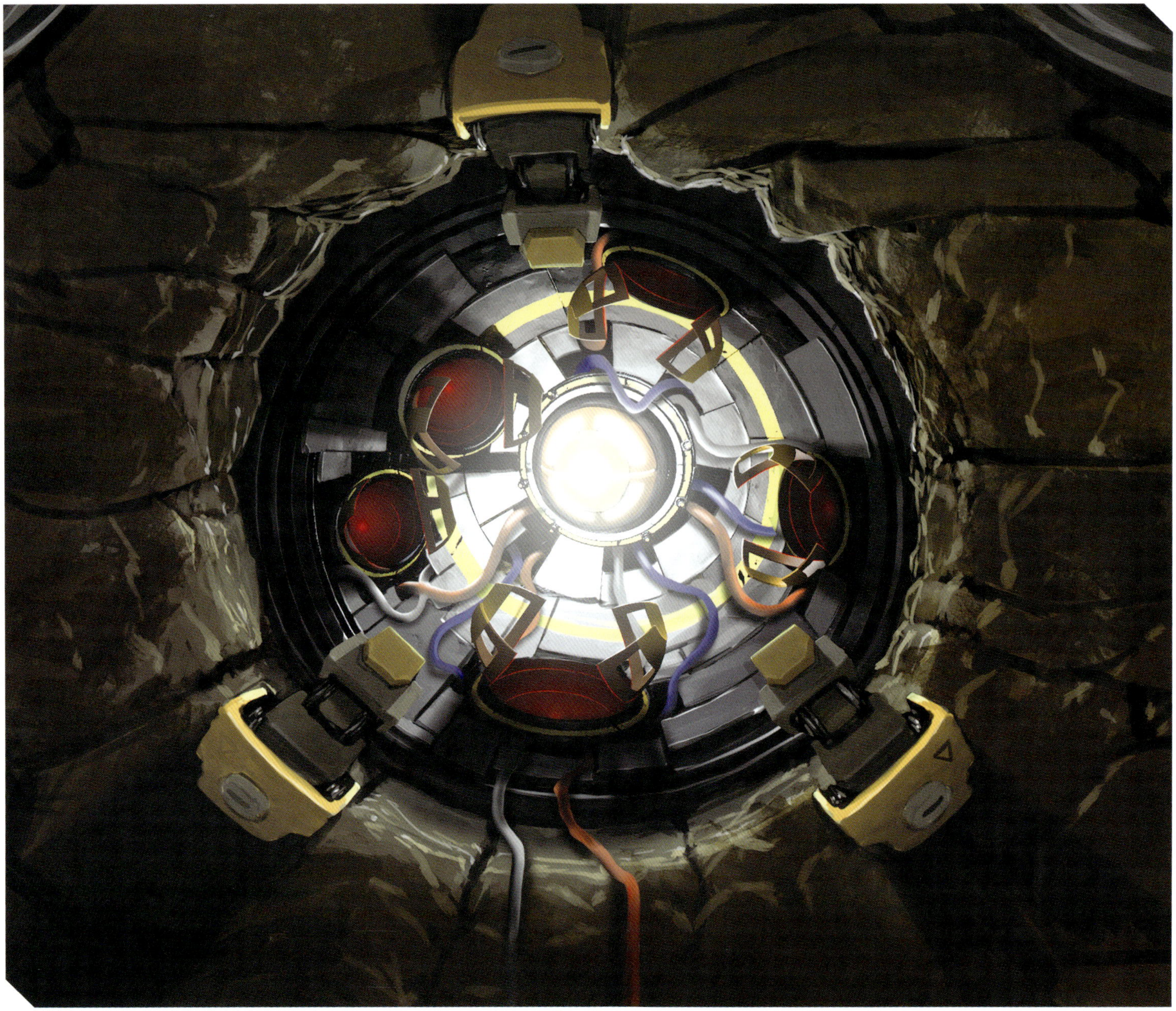

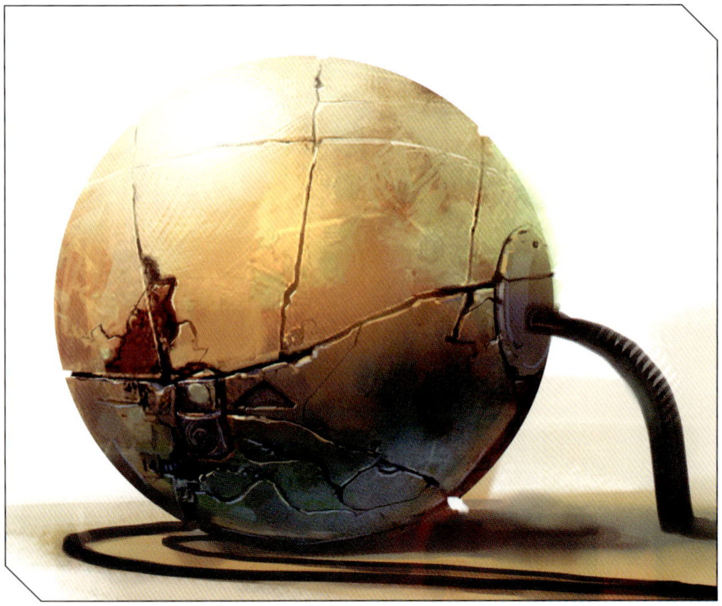

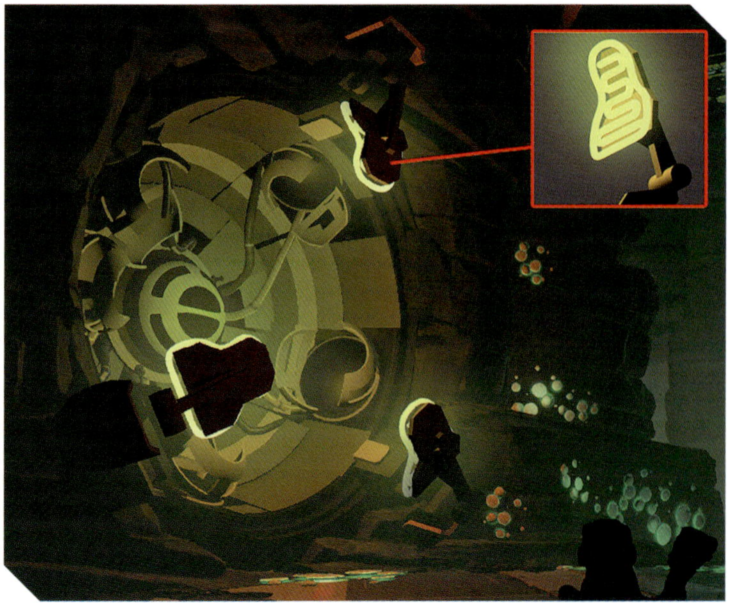

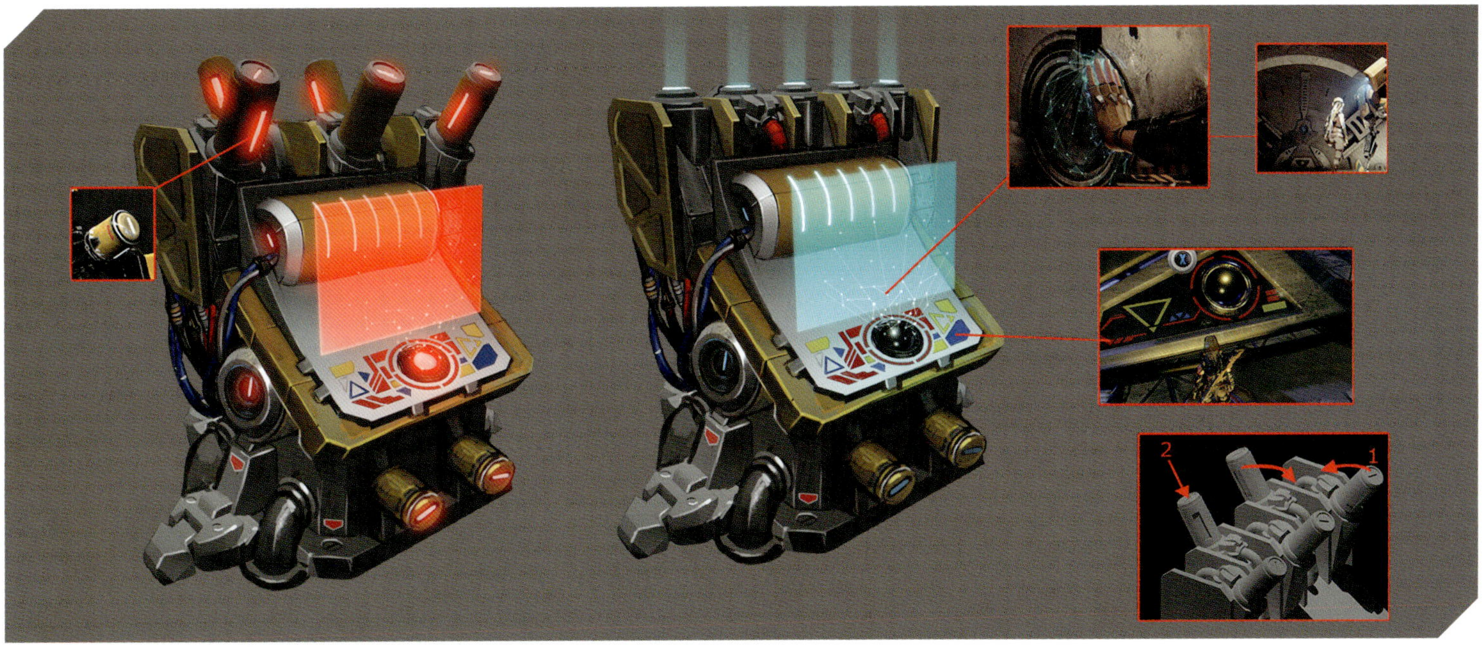
2
1

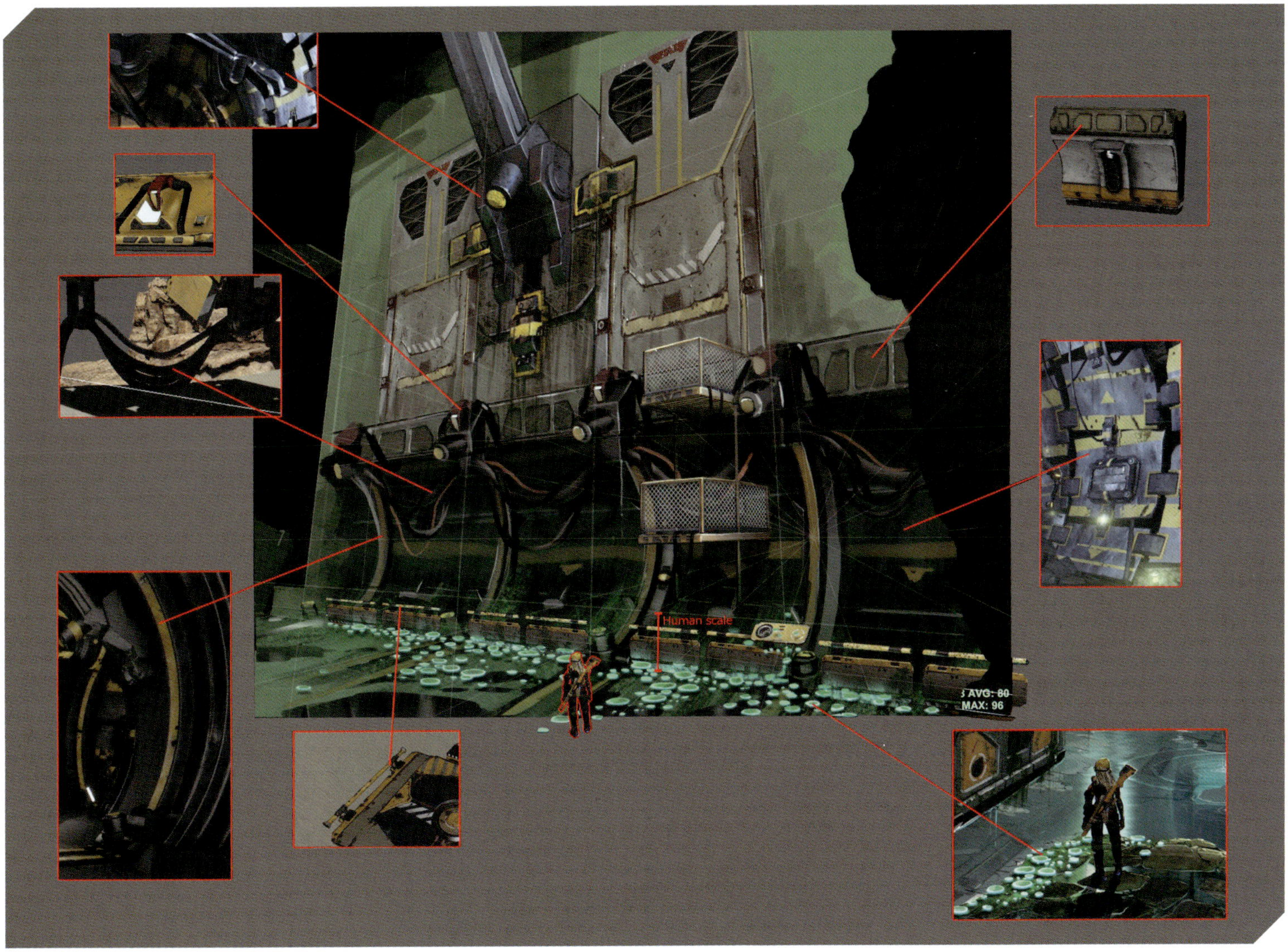
Human scale
AVG: 80
MAX: 96

Damien Papet

On the facing page is a Core Incubator, where the AI personalities are baked into the Cores. Above are explorations of the control consoles that Joule uses to interact with vital foundry machinery.

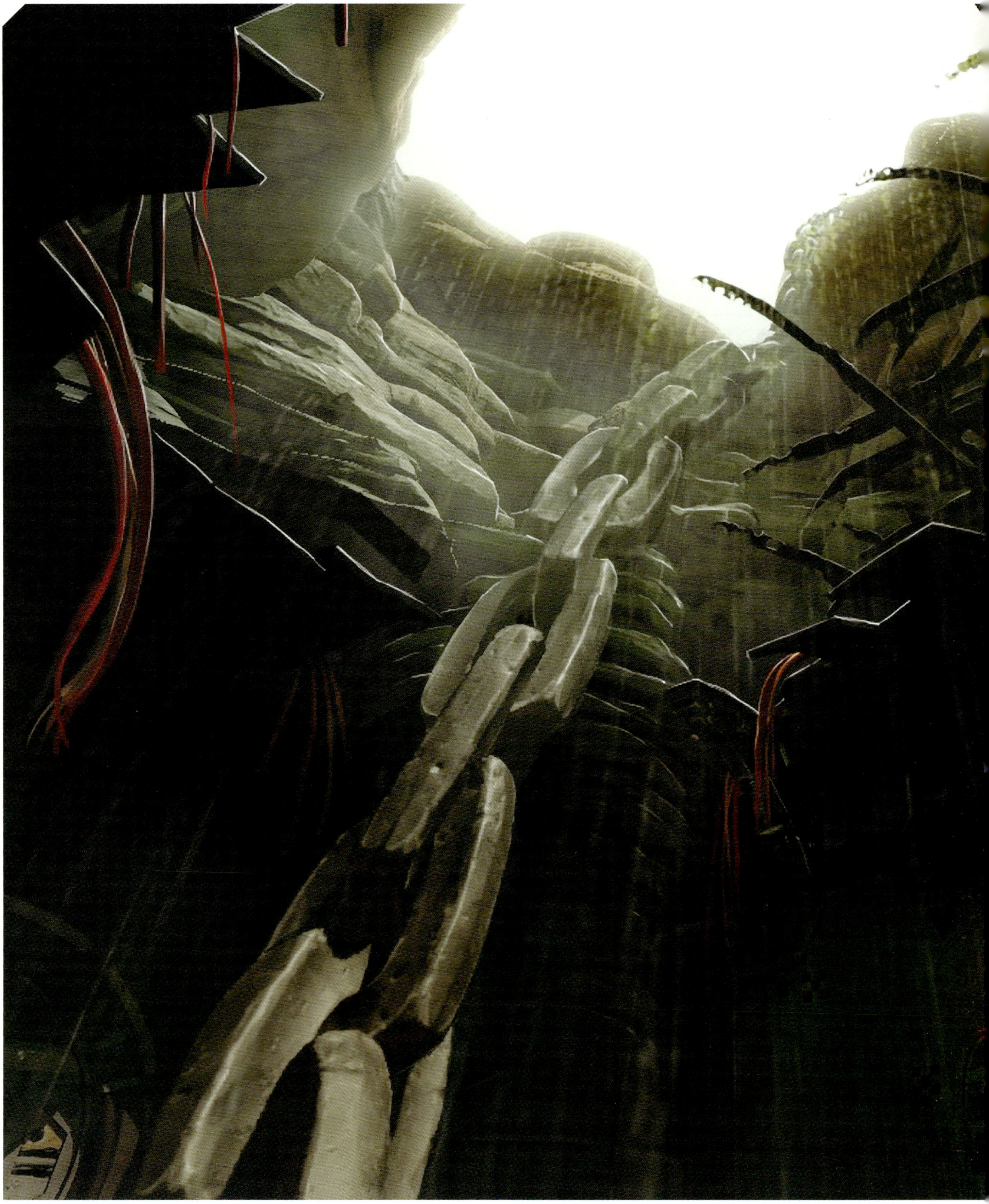

Damien Papet

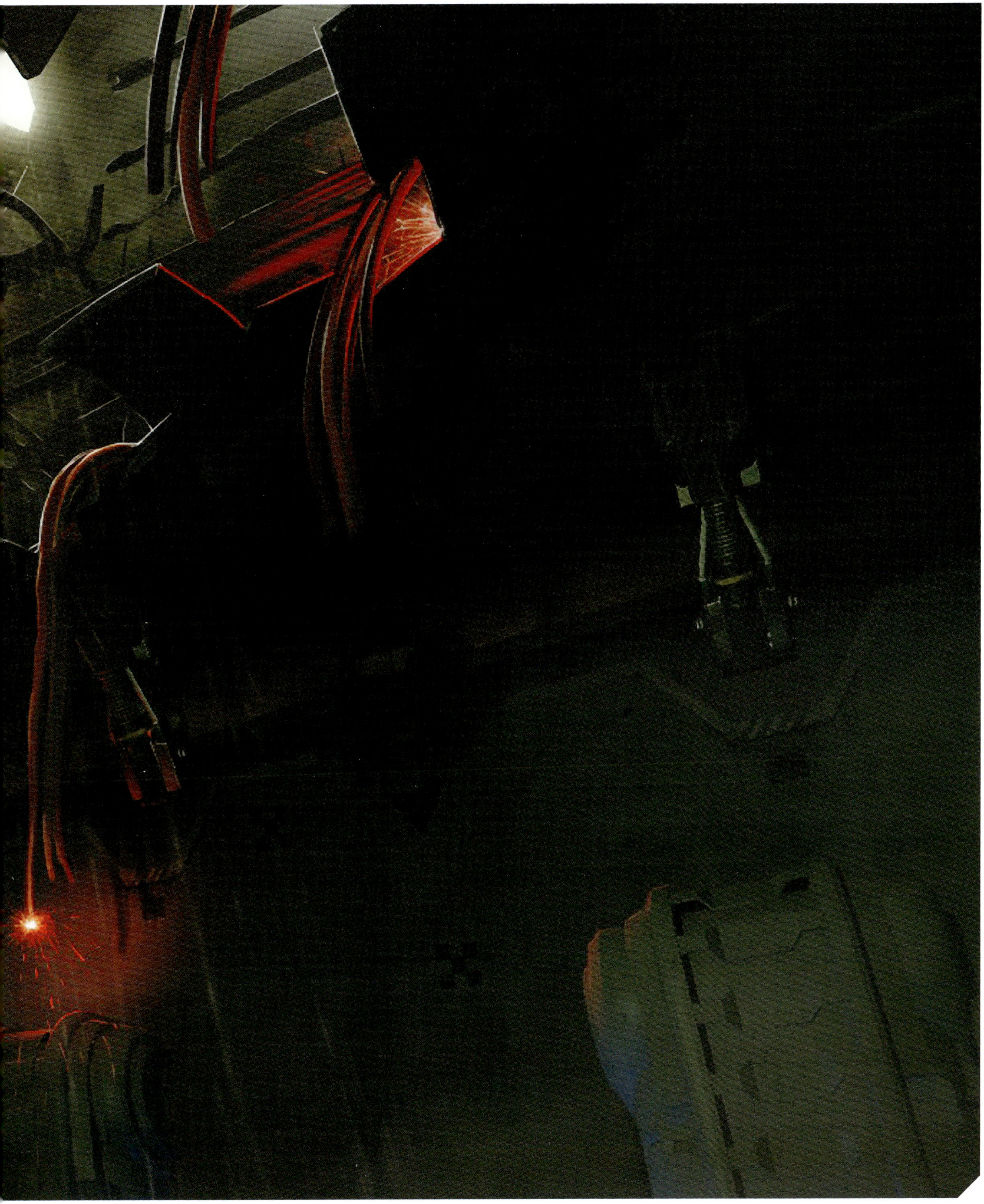

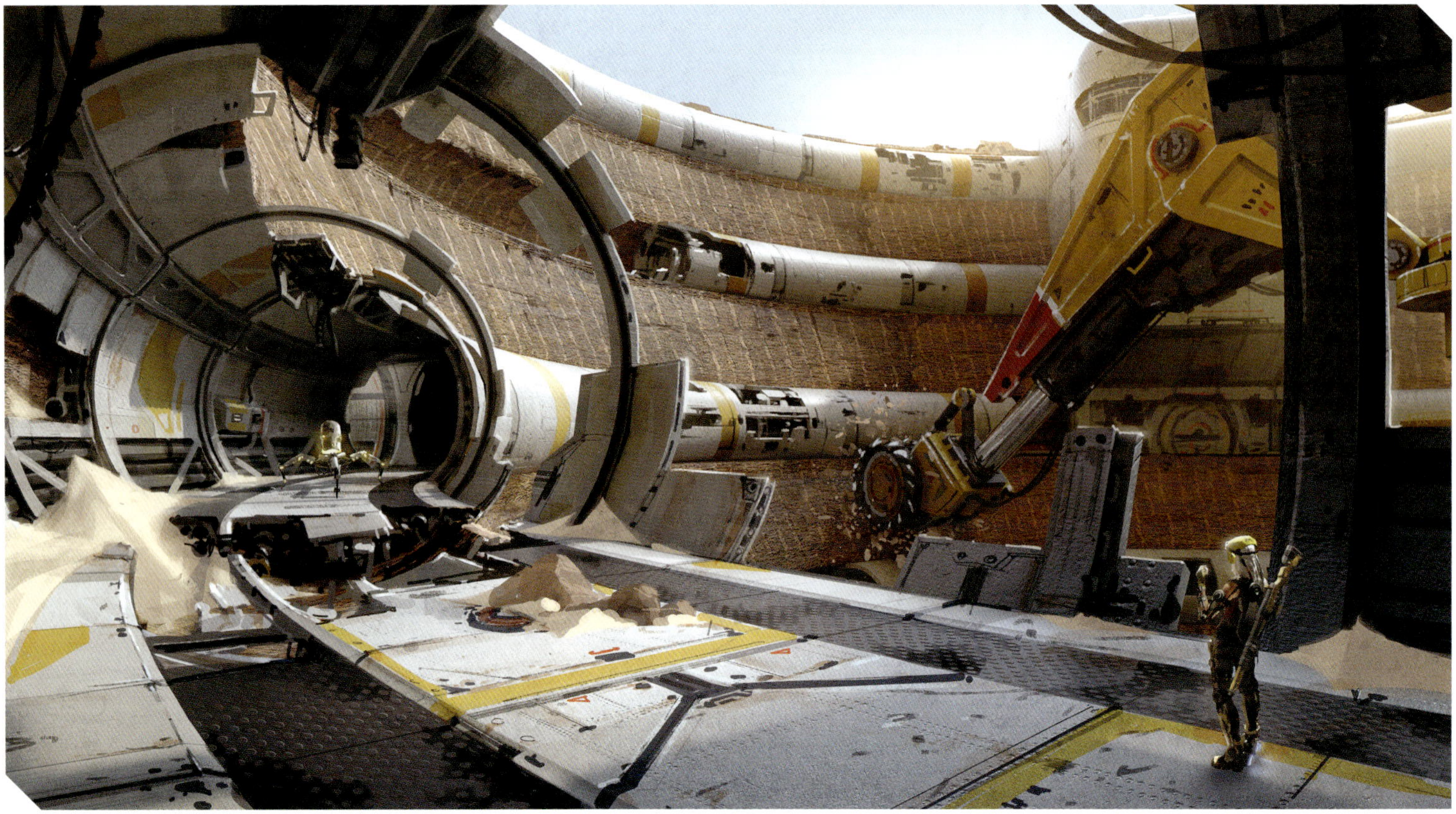

THE QUARRY

An excavation pit dominates one of the game's explorable areas. Here a hulking drill mines the rare crystalline materials essential to the Core manufacturing process.

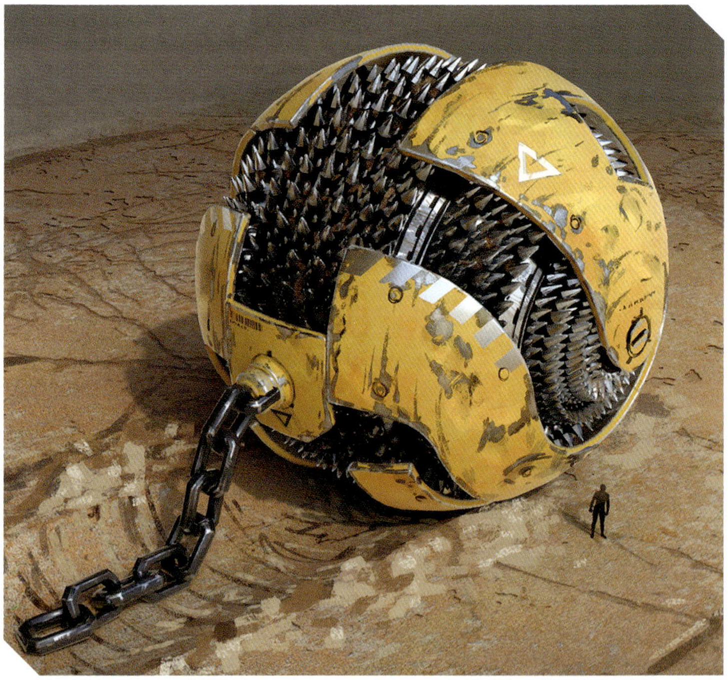

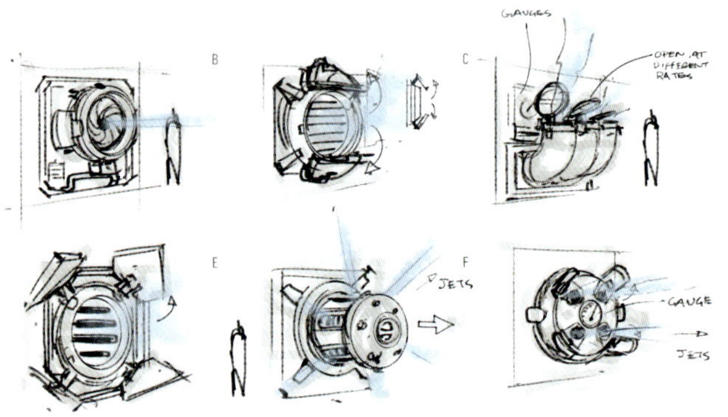

B
C
GAUGES
OPEN AT DIFFERENT RATES
E
F
JETS
GAUGE
JETS

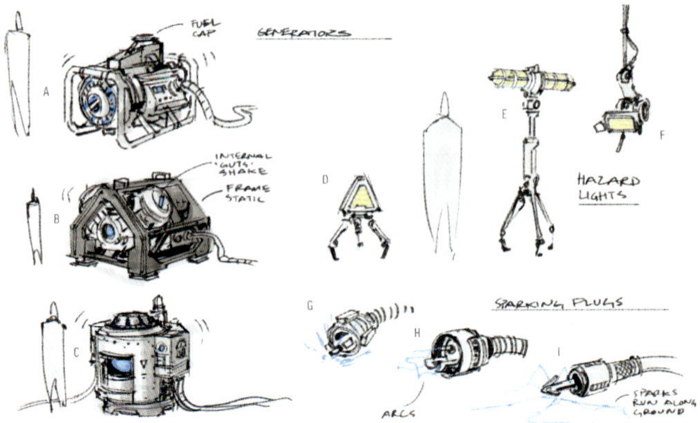

FUEL CAP
GENERATORS
A
INTERNAL GUTS SHAKE
FRAME STATIC
B
C
D
E
F
HAZARD LIGHTS
G
H
I
SPARKING PLUGS
ARCS
SPARKS RUN ALONG GROUND

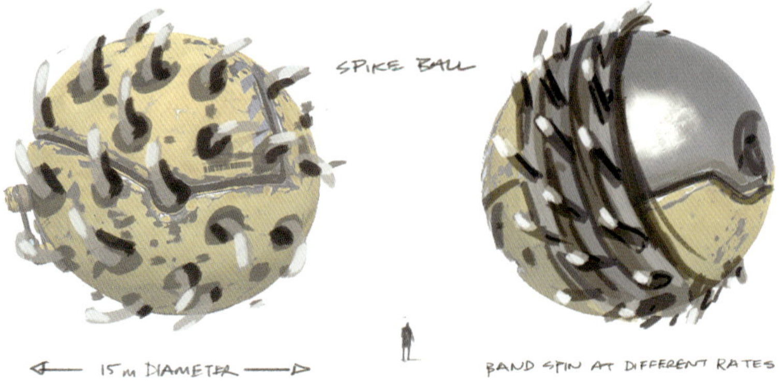

SPIKE BALL
15 m DIAMETER
BAND SPIN AT DIFFERENT RATES

Ryan Denning

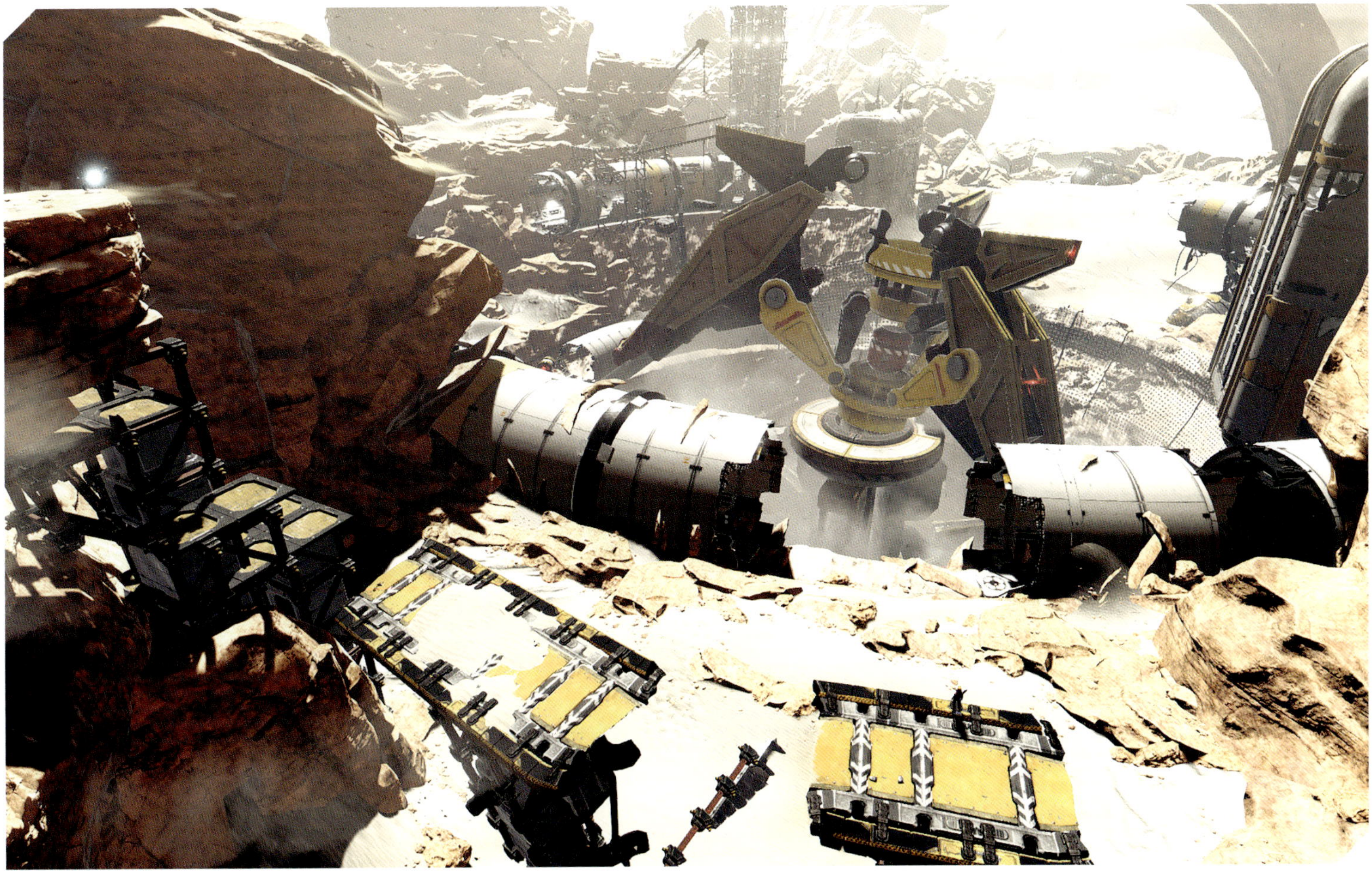

Alexis Boyer, Chris Percle, Elizabeth Foster, Kip Carbone, Markel Milanes, Patrick Sullivan, and Todd Keller

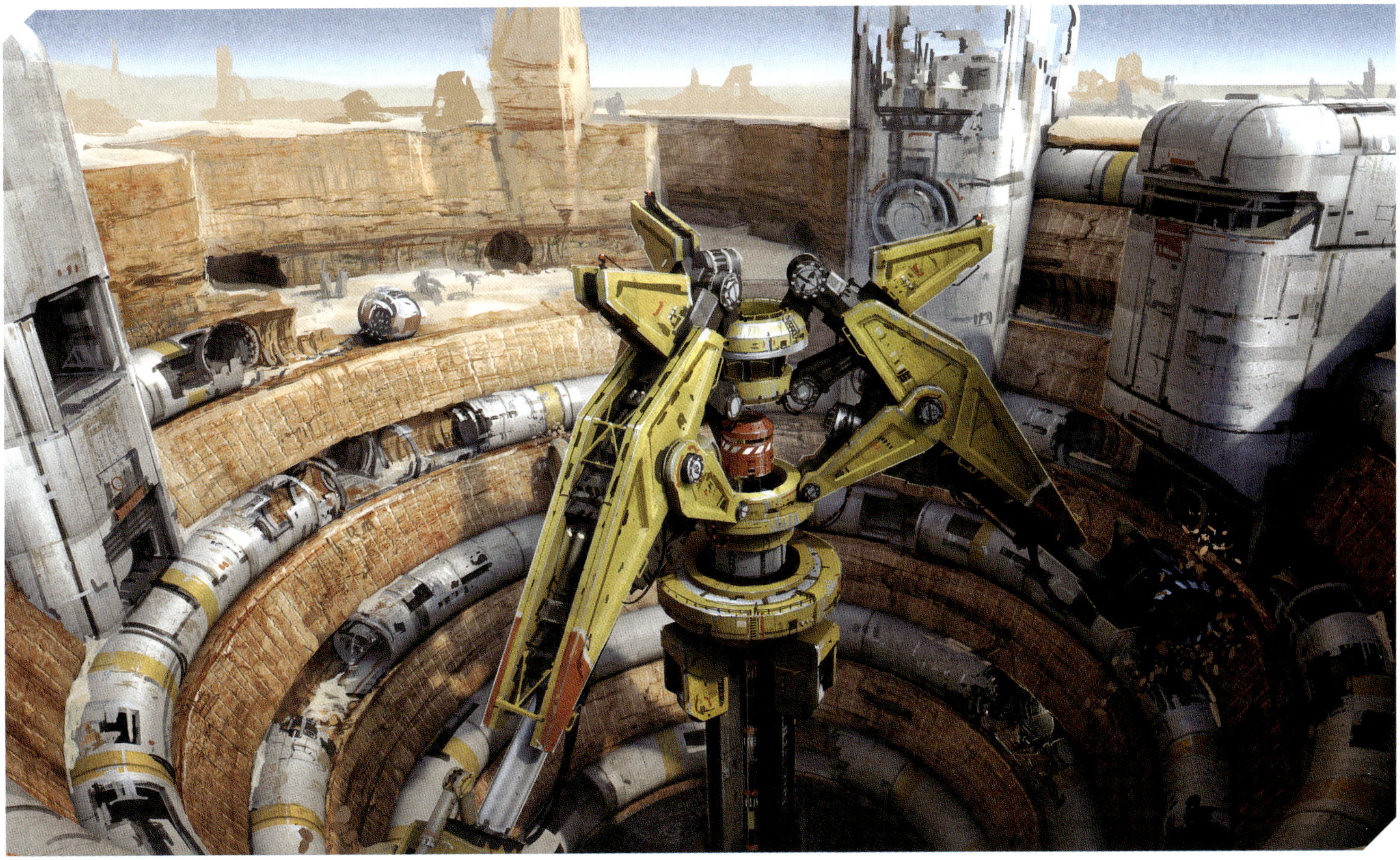

Ryan Denning

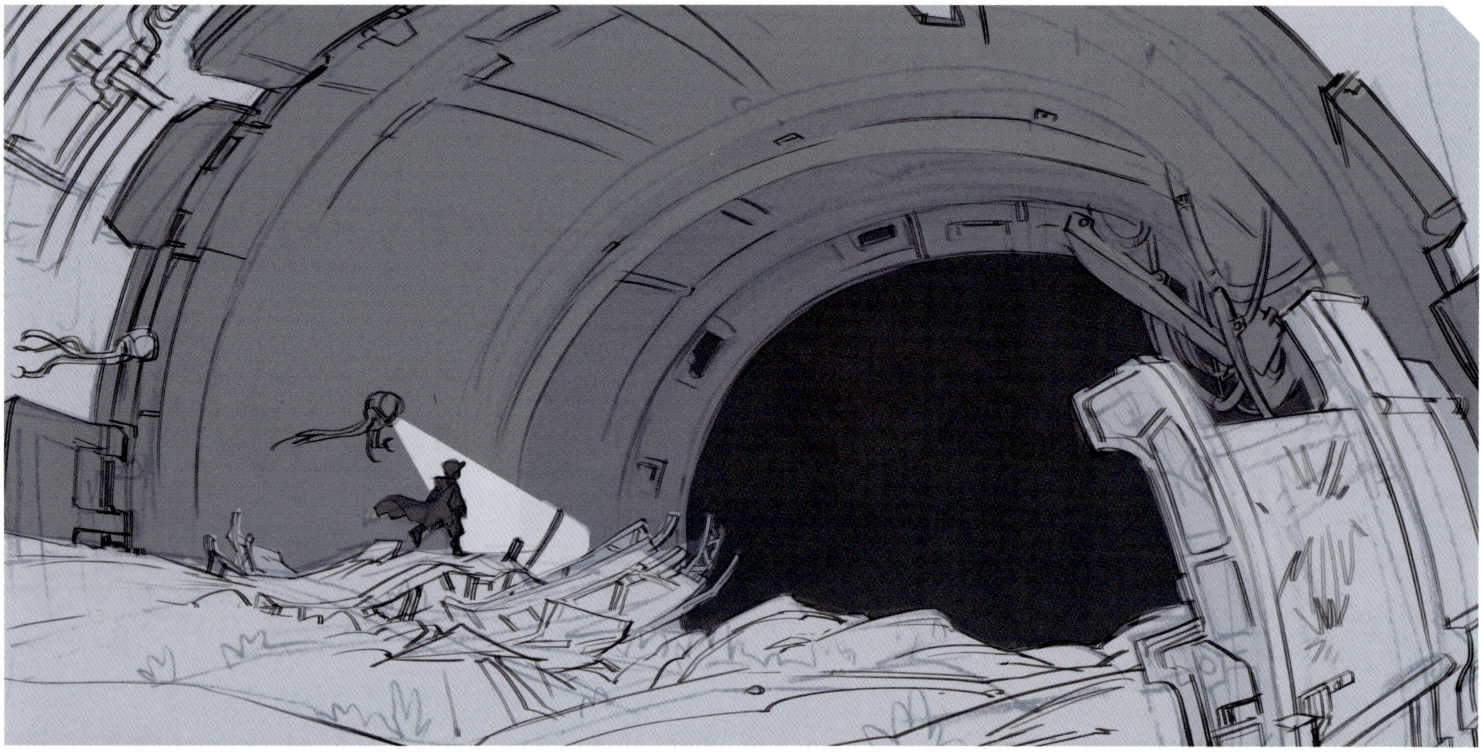

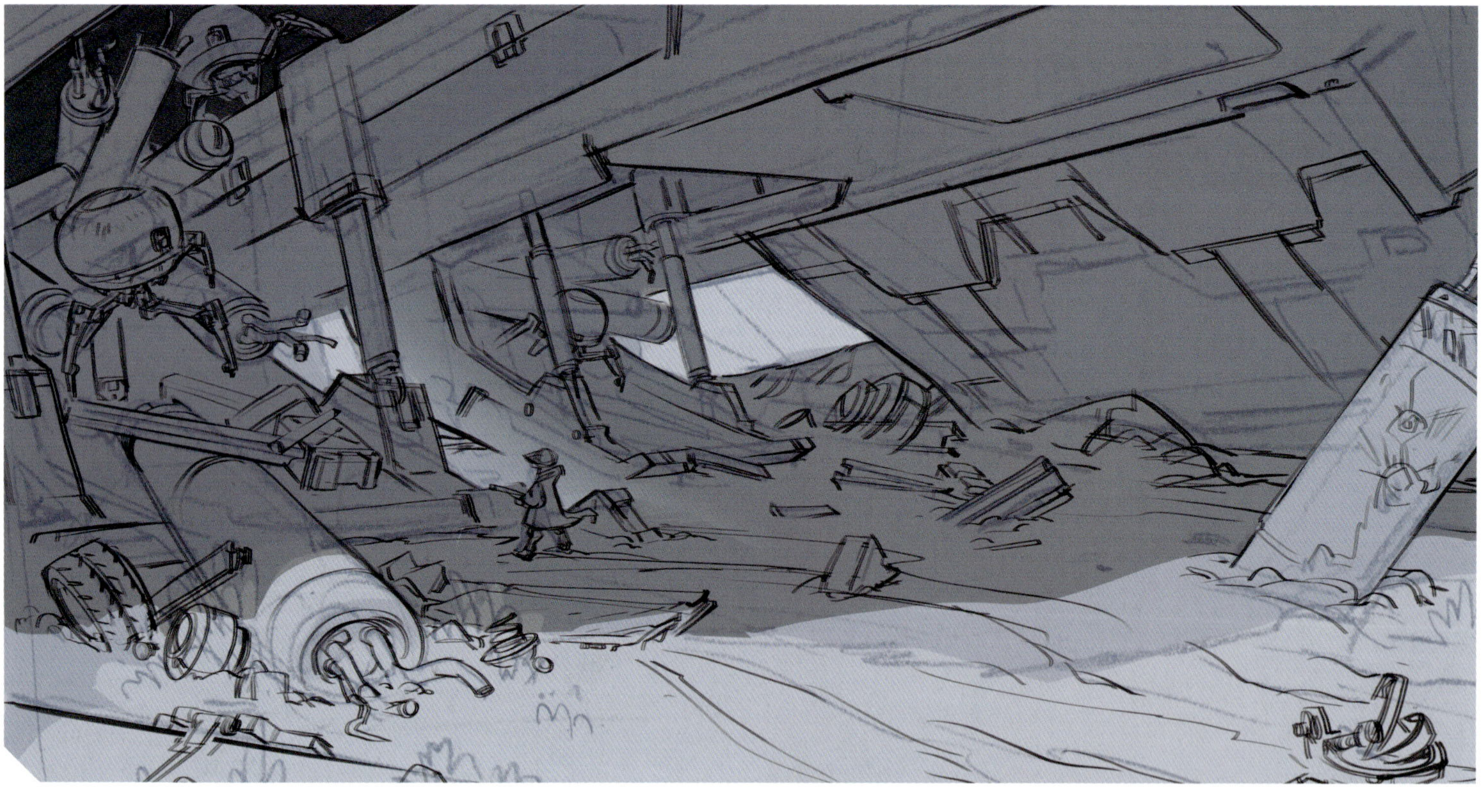

THE CRASH SITE

Here we give the player a glimpse of the tragic end of one of the human evacuation ships after an attack by Victor. The scale of this vessel, like other key landmarks in *ReCore*, is huge.

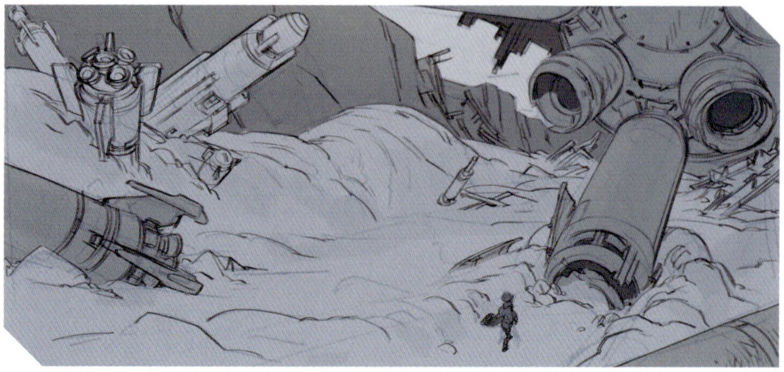

Paul Richards

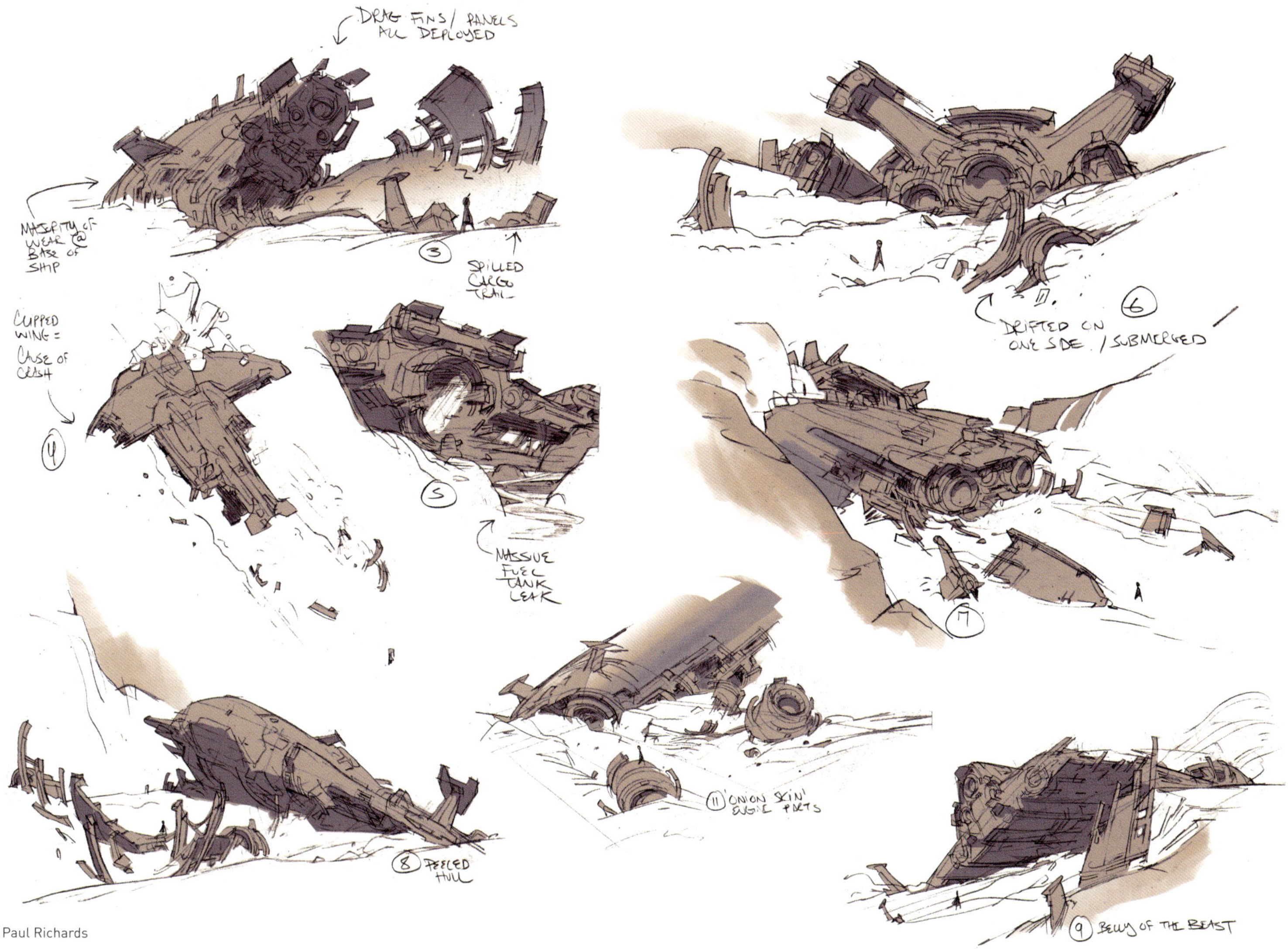
DRAG FINS / PANELS ALL DEPLOYED
MAJORITY OF WEAR @ BASE OF SHIP
3
SPILLED CARGO TRAIL
6
DRIFTED ON ONE SIDE / SUBMERGED
CLIPPED WING = CAUSE OF CRASH
4
5
MASSIVE FUEL TANK LEAK
7
11 'ONION SKIN' ENGINE PARTS
8 PEELED HULL
9 BELLY OF THE BEAST

Paul Richards

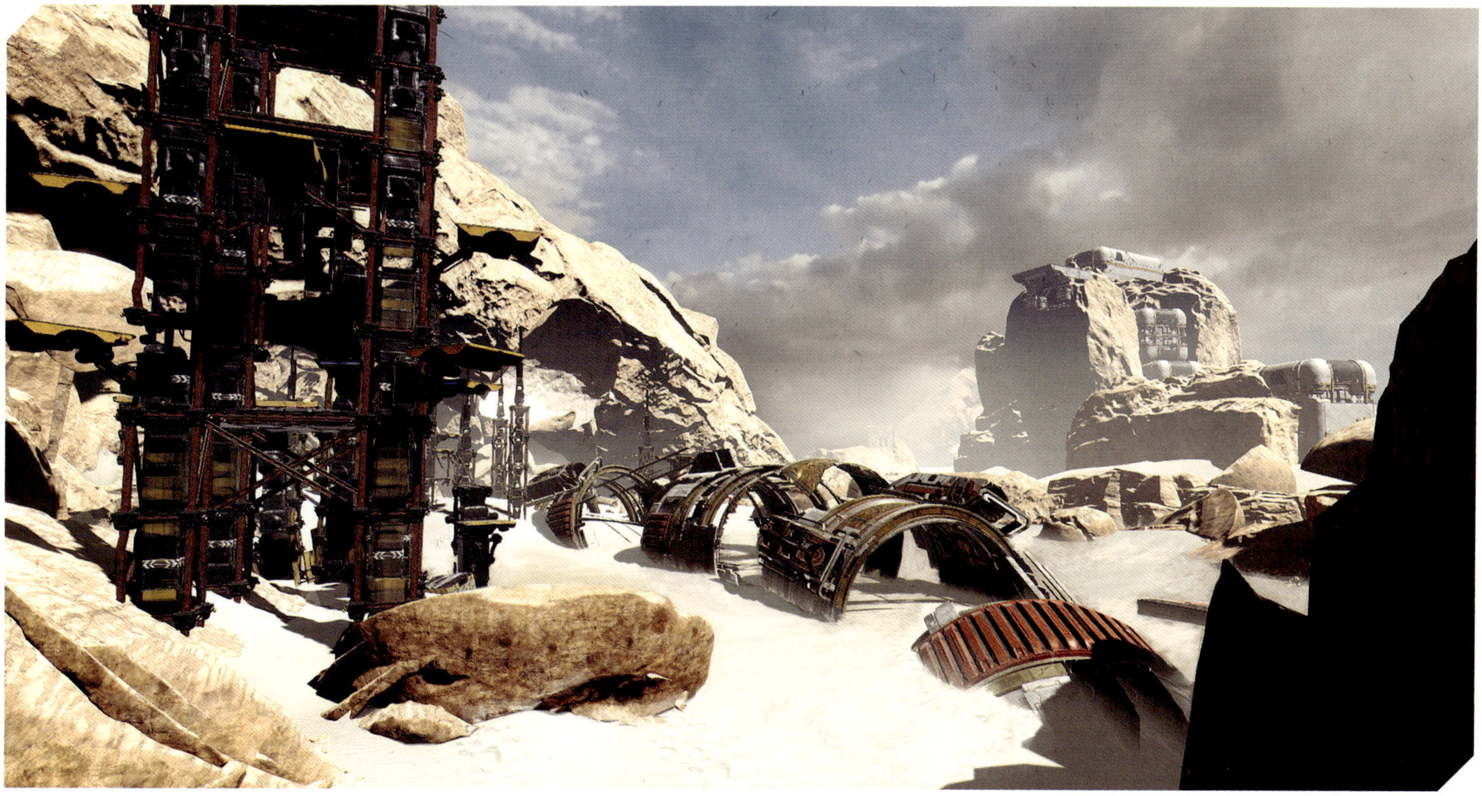

Alexis Boyer, Chris Percle, Elizabeth Foster, Kip Carbone, Markel Milanes, Patrick Sullivan, and Todd Keller

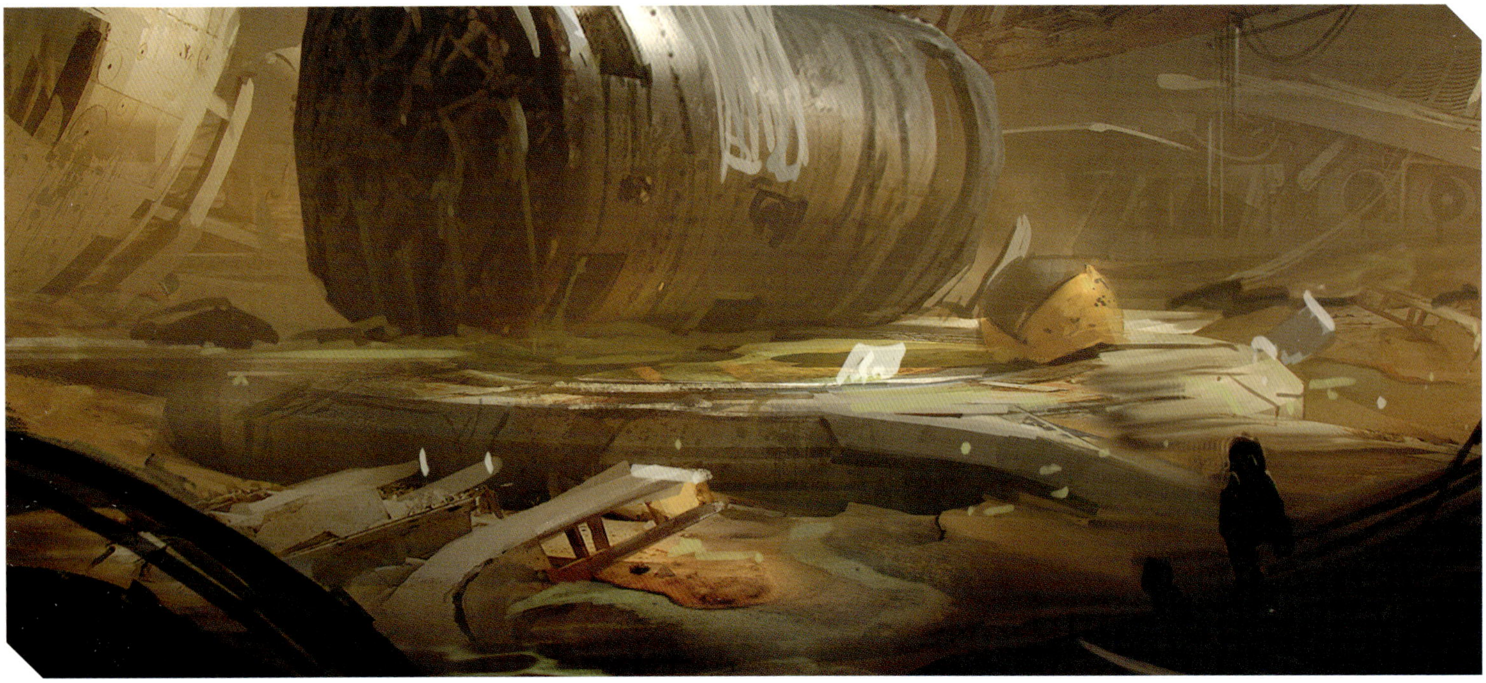

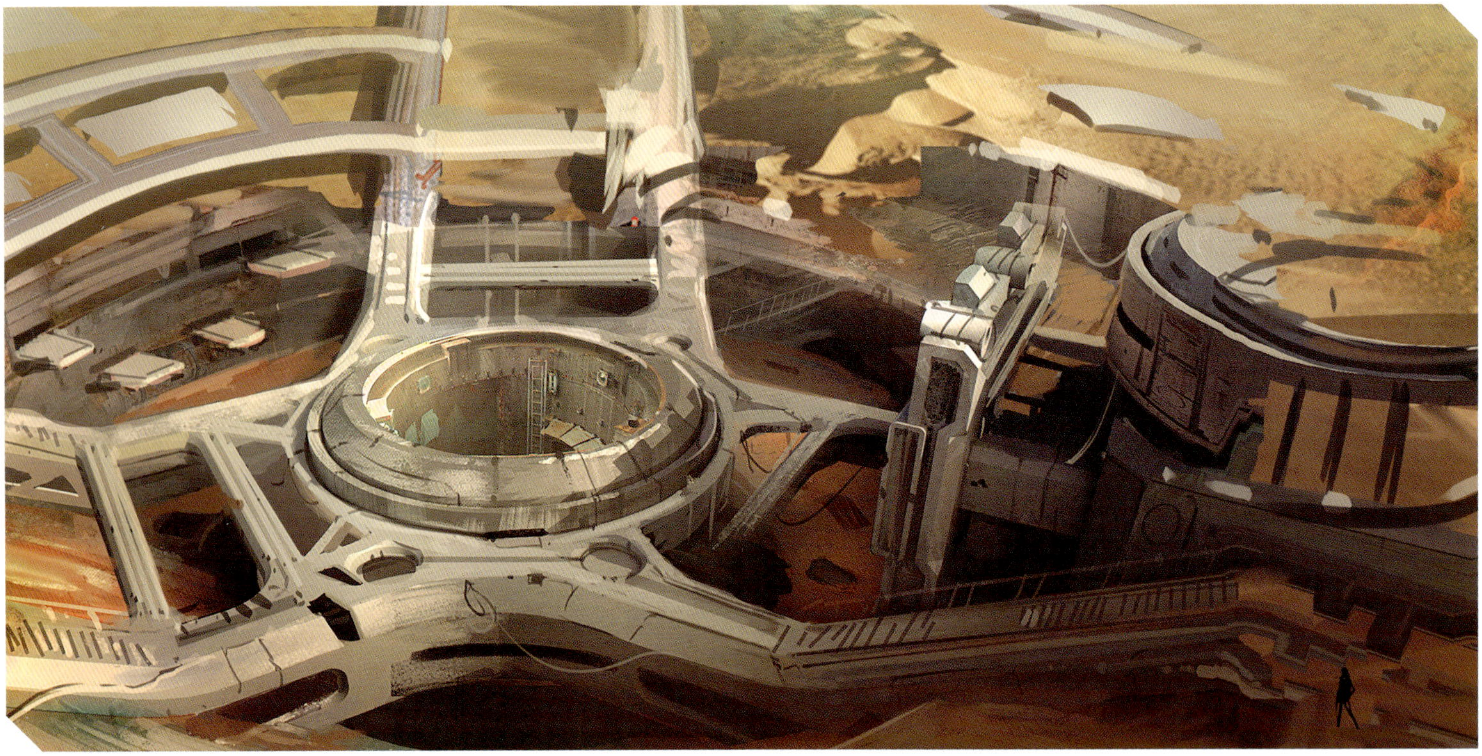

LAUNCH AREA

Centuries of sandstorms have taken their toll on this launch silo for a rocket designed to ferry passengers and equipment from the surface to orbit. We wanted the facility to feel as though it was going to see heavy use by the colonists on Far Eden. There's a slickness to the design that isn't found in structures meant for the Corebots.

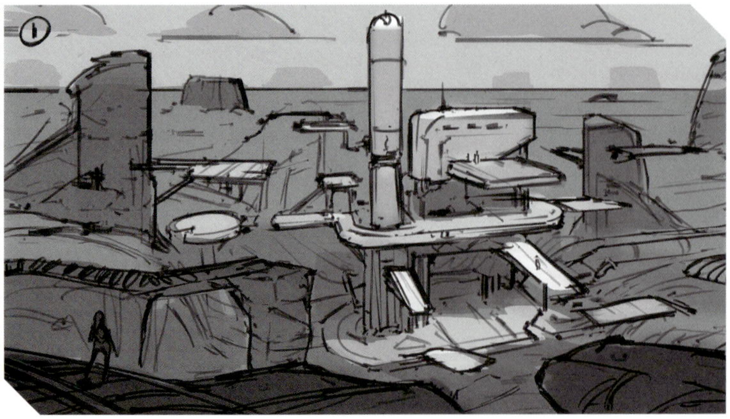

Marcel van Vuuren of Atomhawk

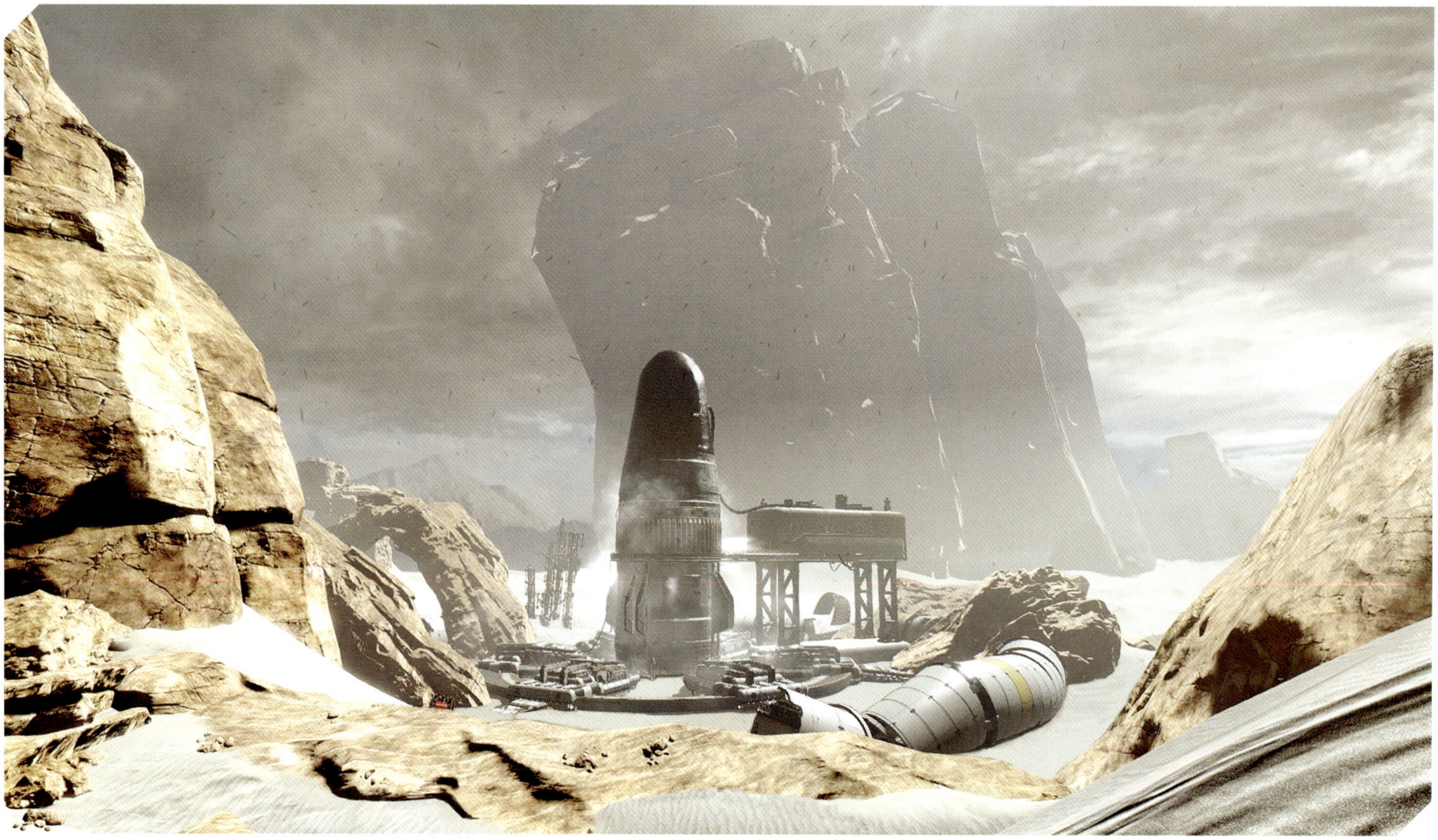

Alexis Boyer, Chris Percle, Elizabeth Foster, Kip Carbone, Markel Milanes, Patrick Sullivan, and Todd Keller

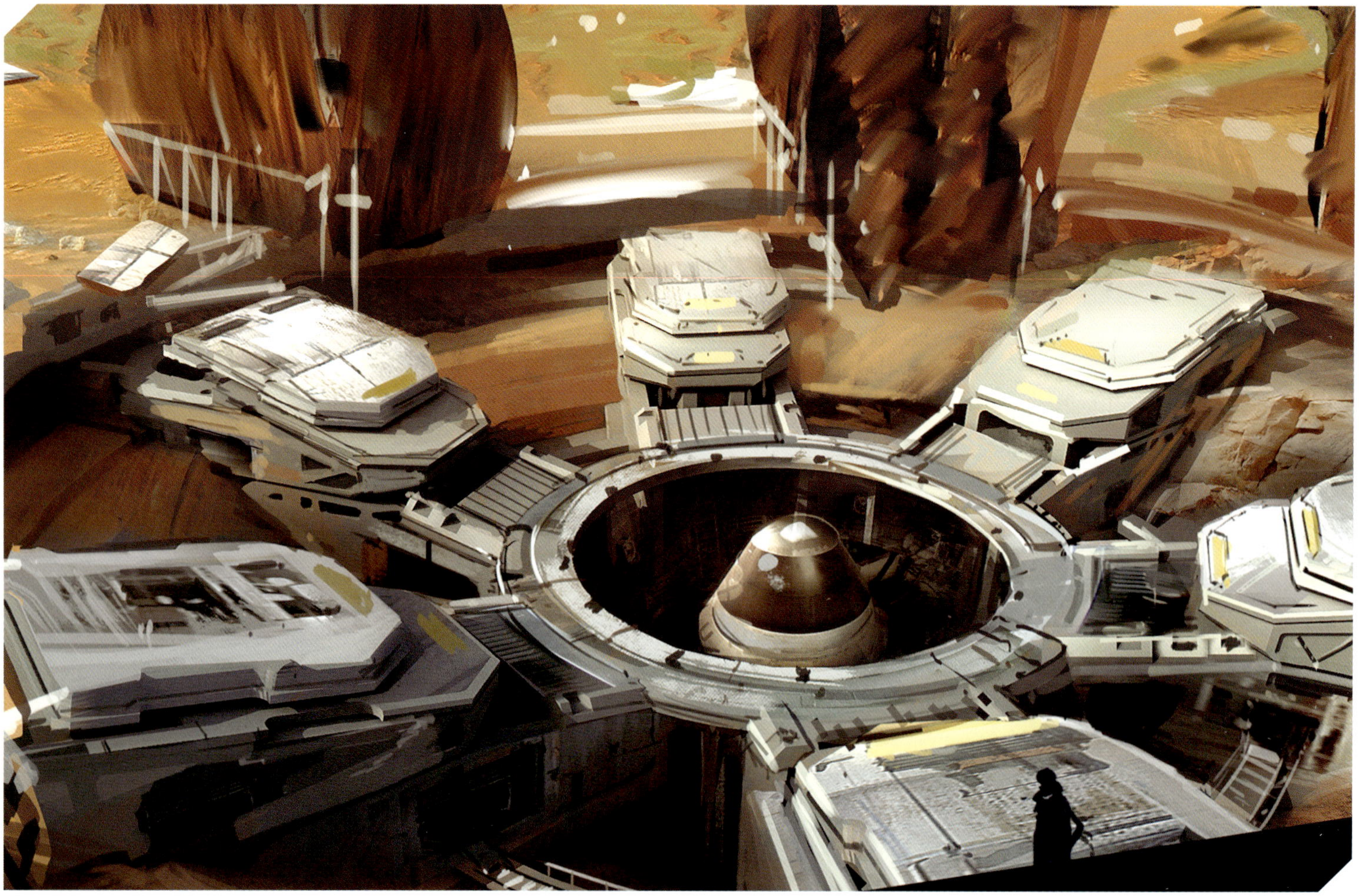

Marcel van Vuuren of Atomhawk

During production, the environment team generally used concepts that were more line-driven. To enhance the mood of an area, the concept artists would create a more polished painting.

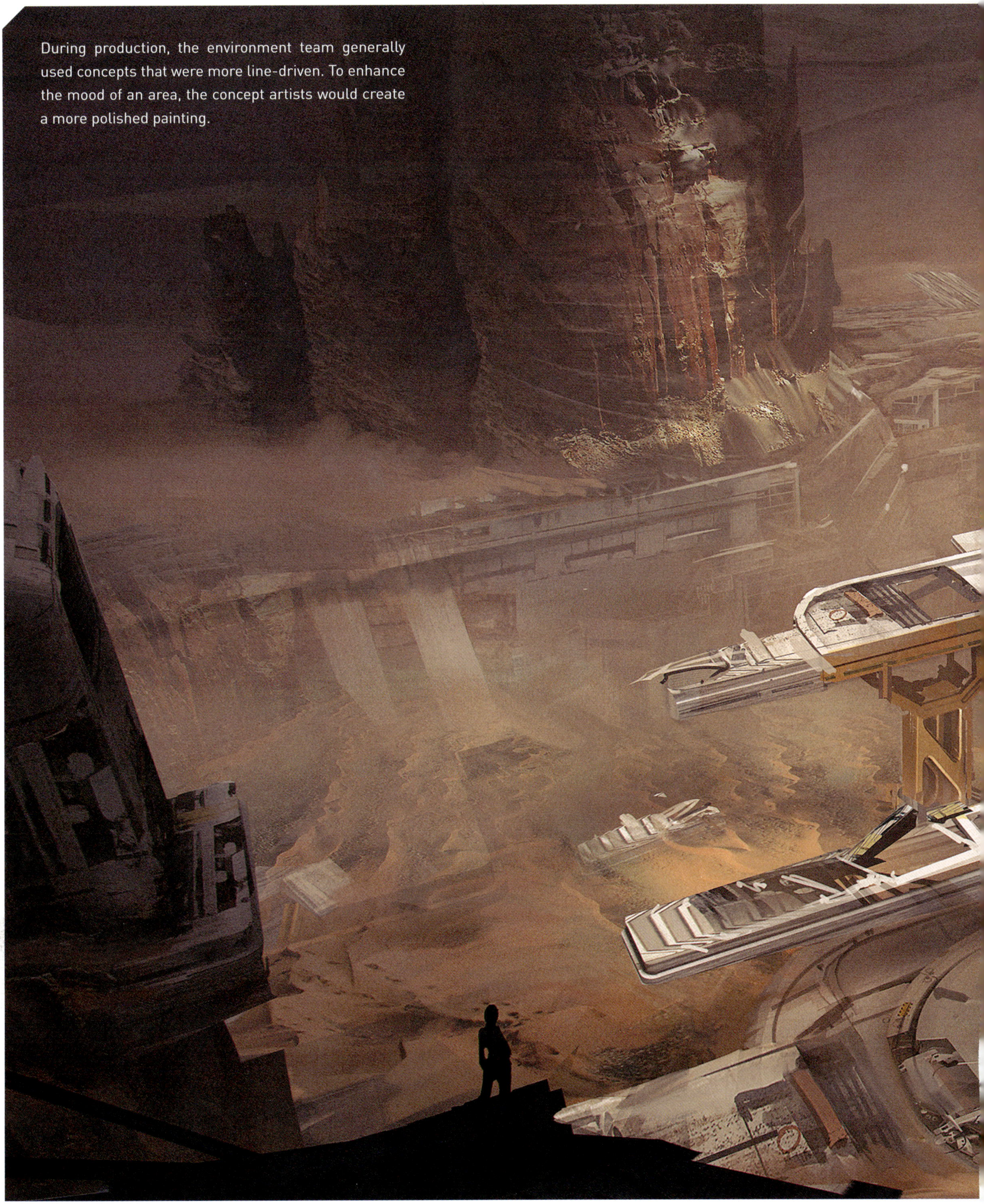

Marcel van Vuuren of Atomhawk

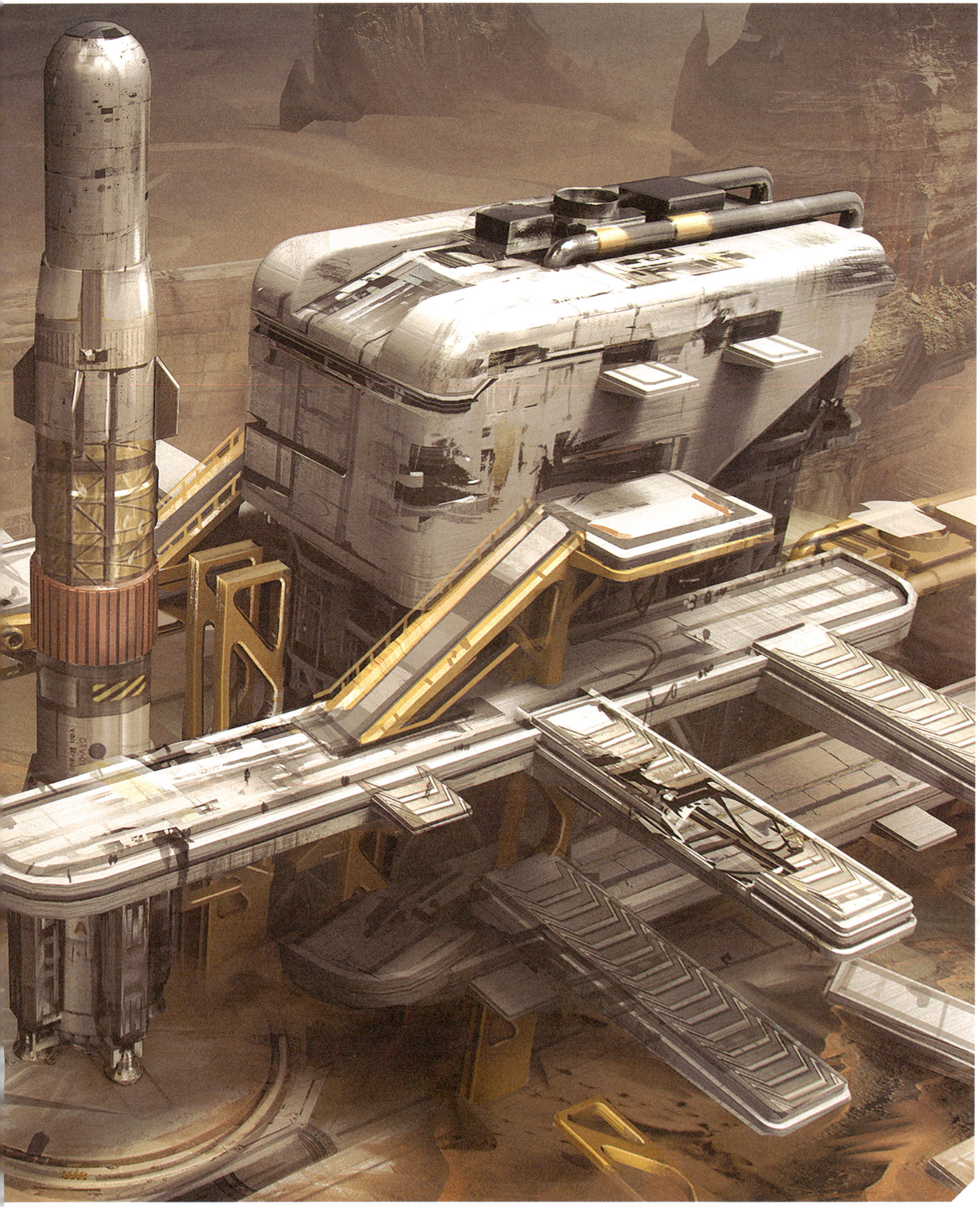

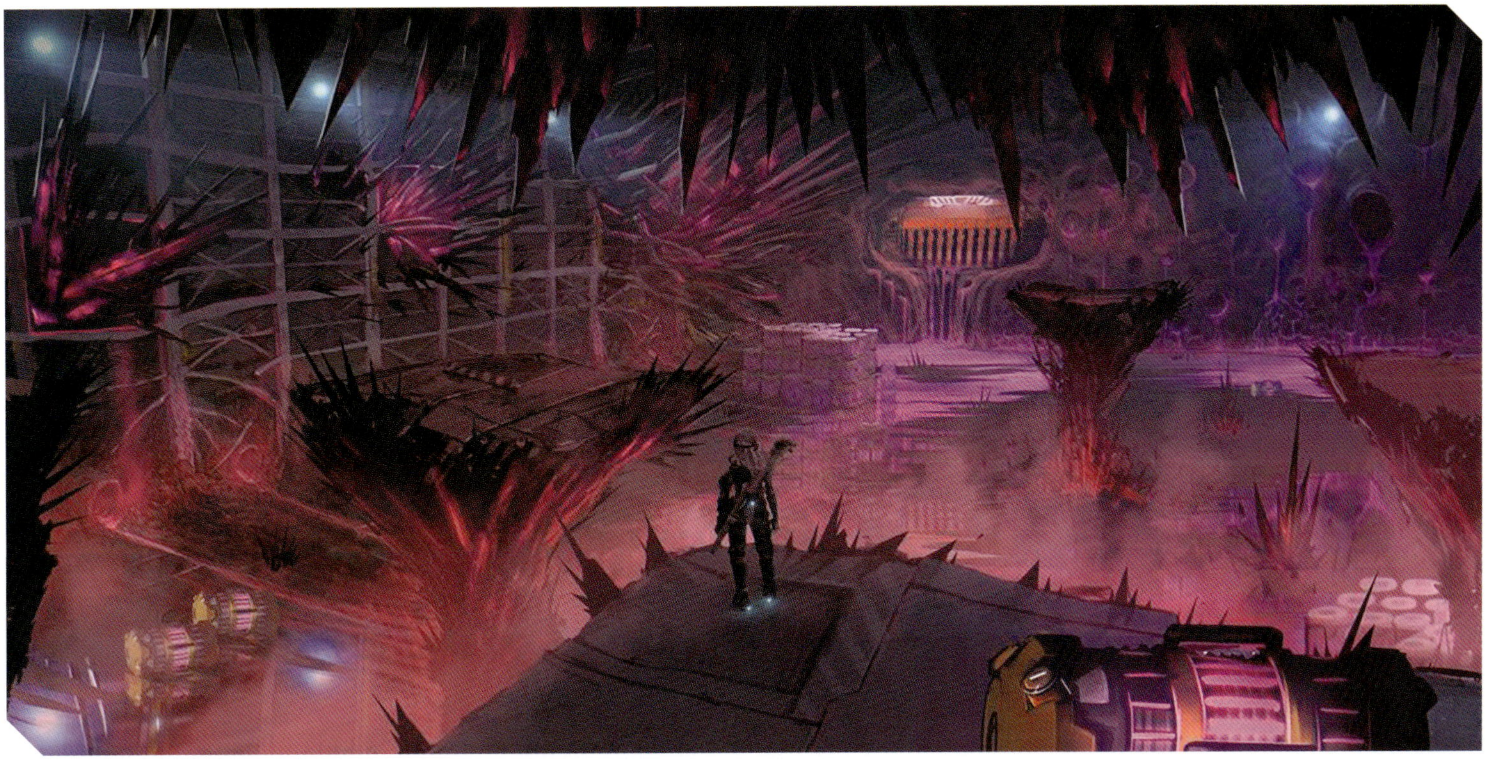

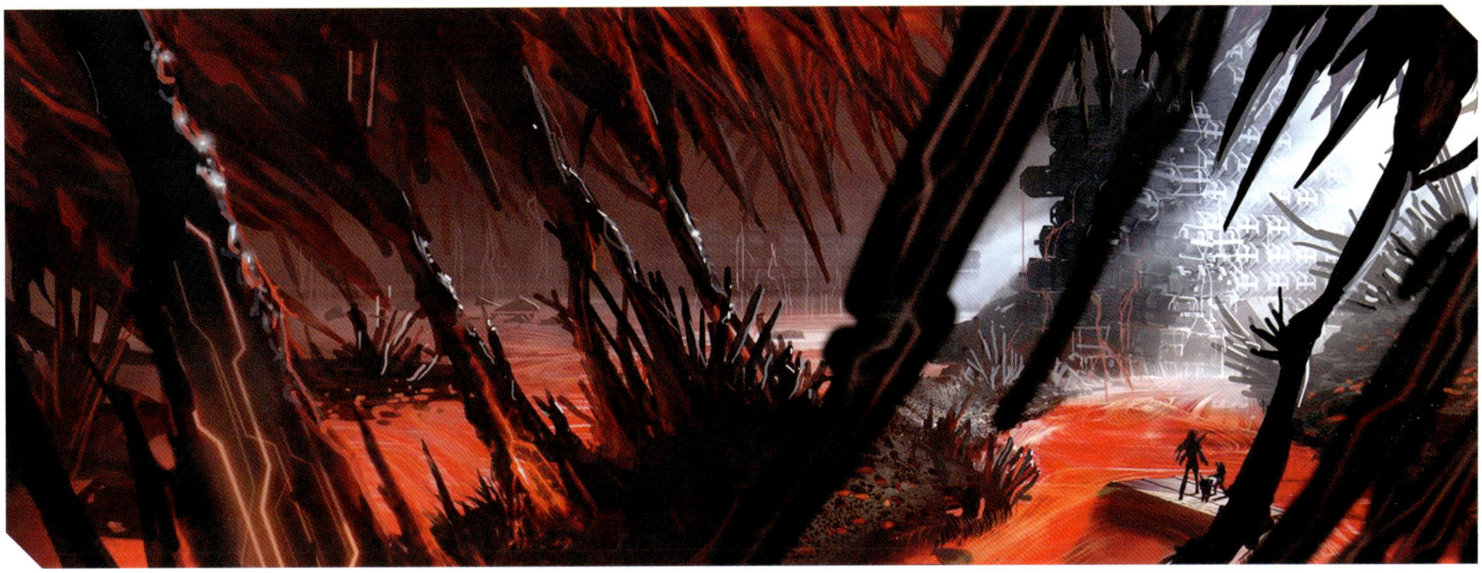

Damien Papet

THE WARREN

These caverns mark the boundary of Victor's domain and echo his corrupting influence on the Corebots. Just as Victor upsets the plans for the Far Eden colony, so too are the objects in these caves chaotic and set at awkward angles. Victor's influence has even polluted the "E-Turner," or Corebot fuel that flows through the caverns. This toxic fluid was meant to create an environmental hazard for the player. But its initial red color felt too much like lava and was eventually changed to green.

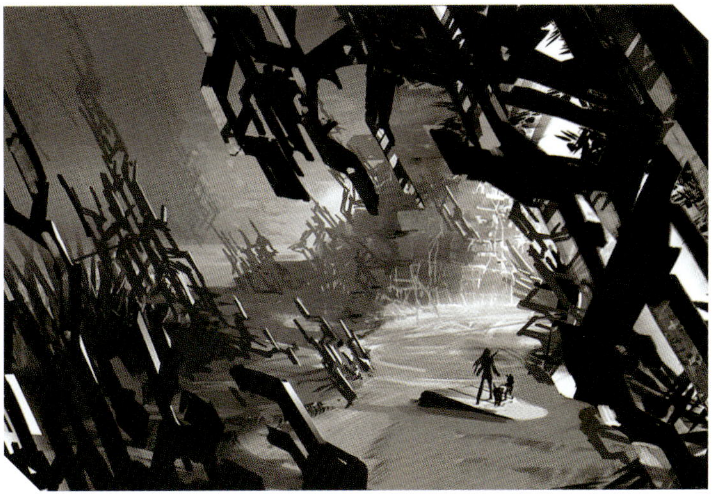

Damien Papet

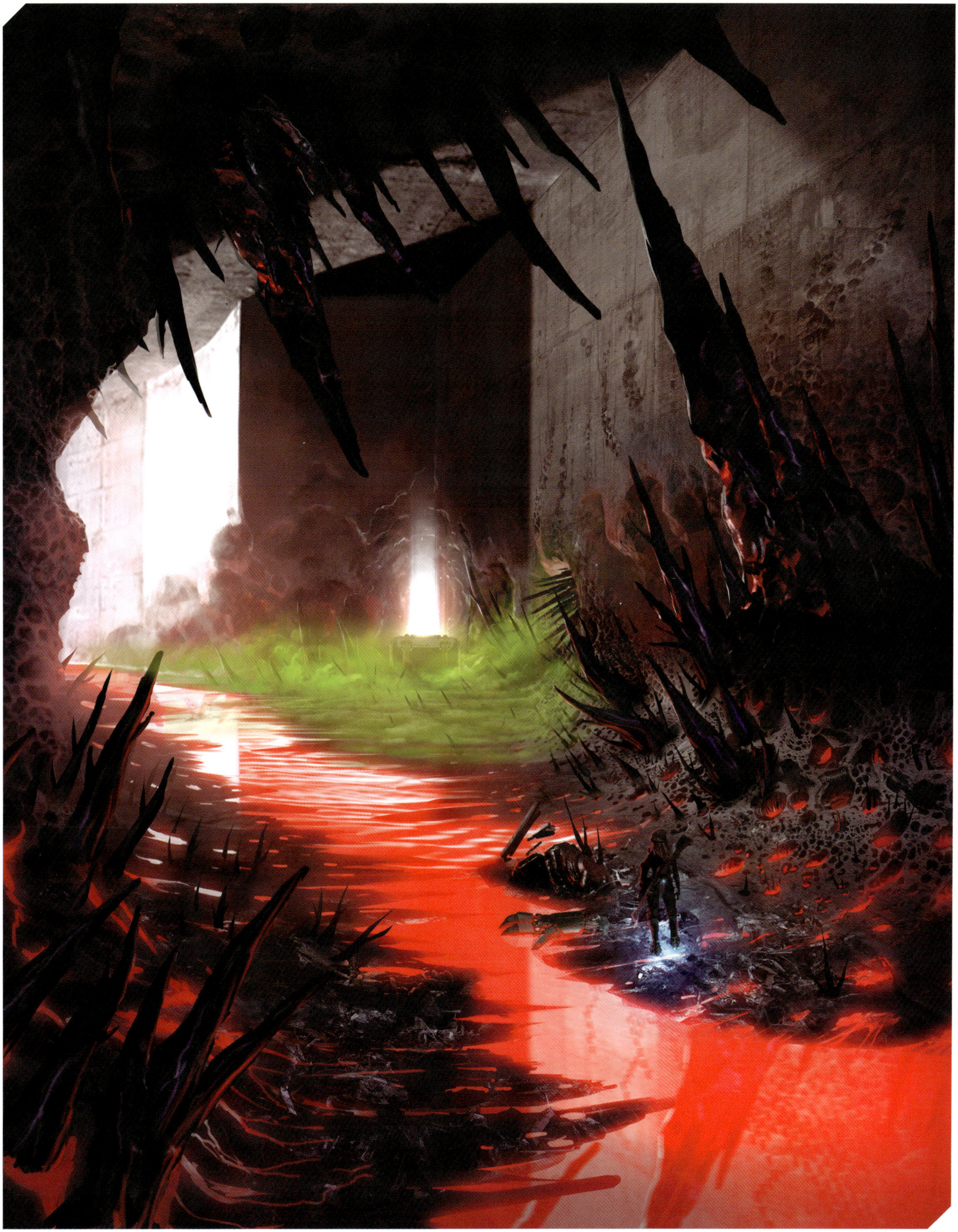

Damien Papet

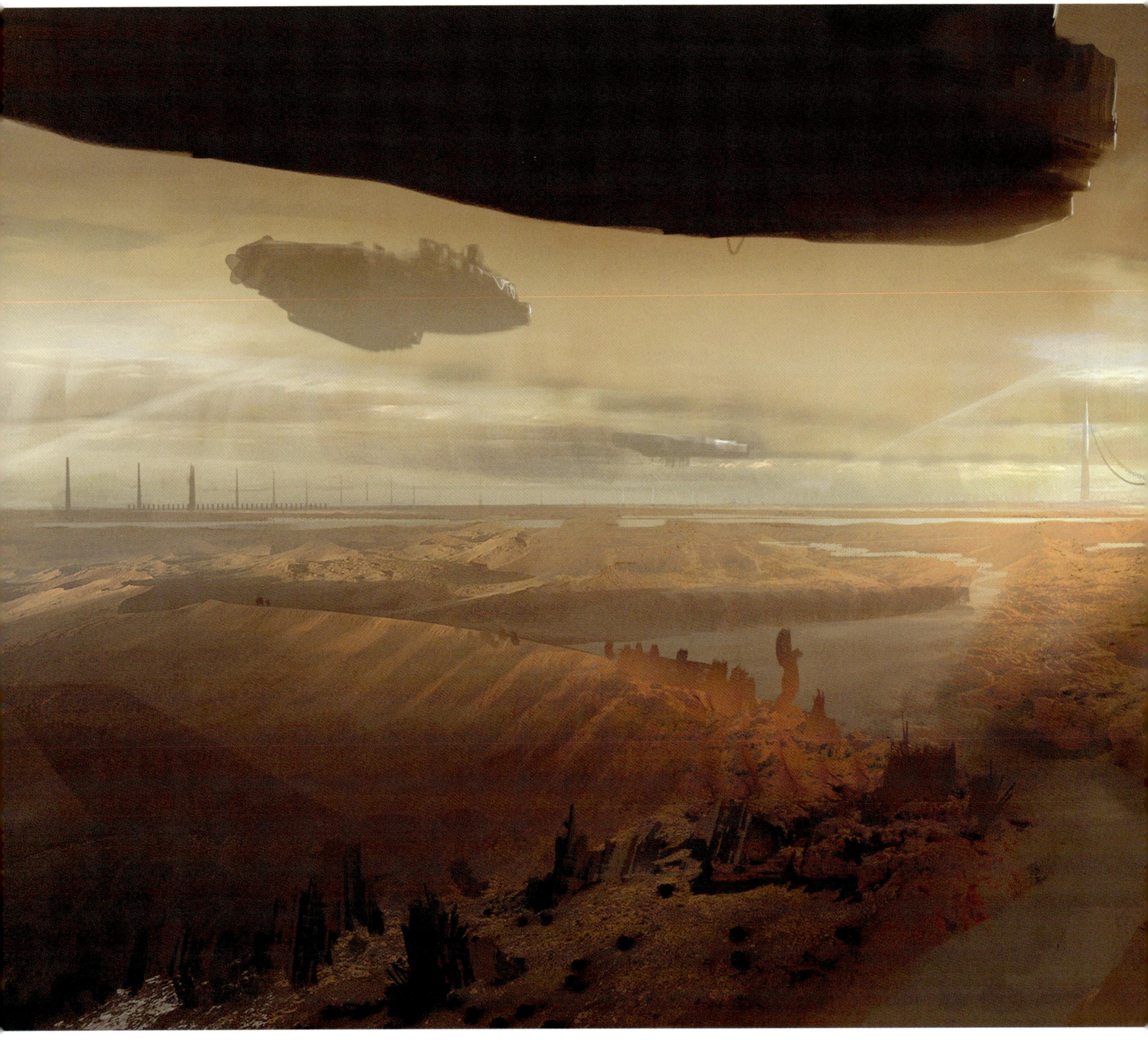

In this early image, Joule emerges from the corrupted caverns to see Far Eden Tower, Victor's fortress and the heart of the terraforming system.

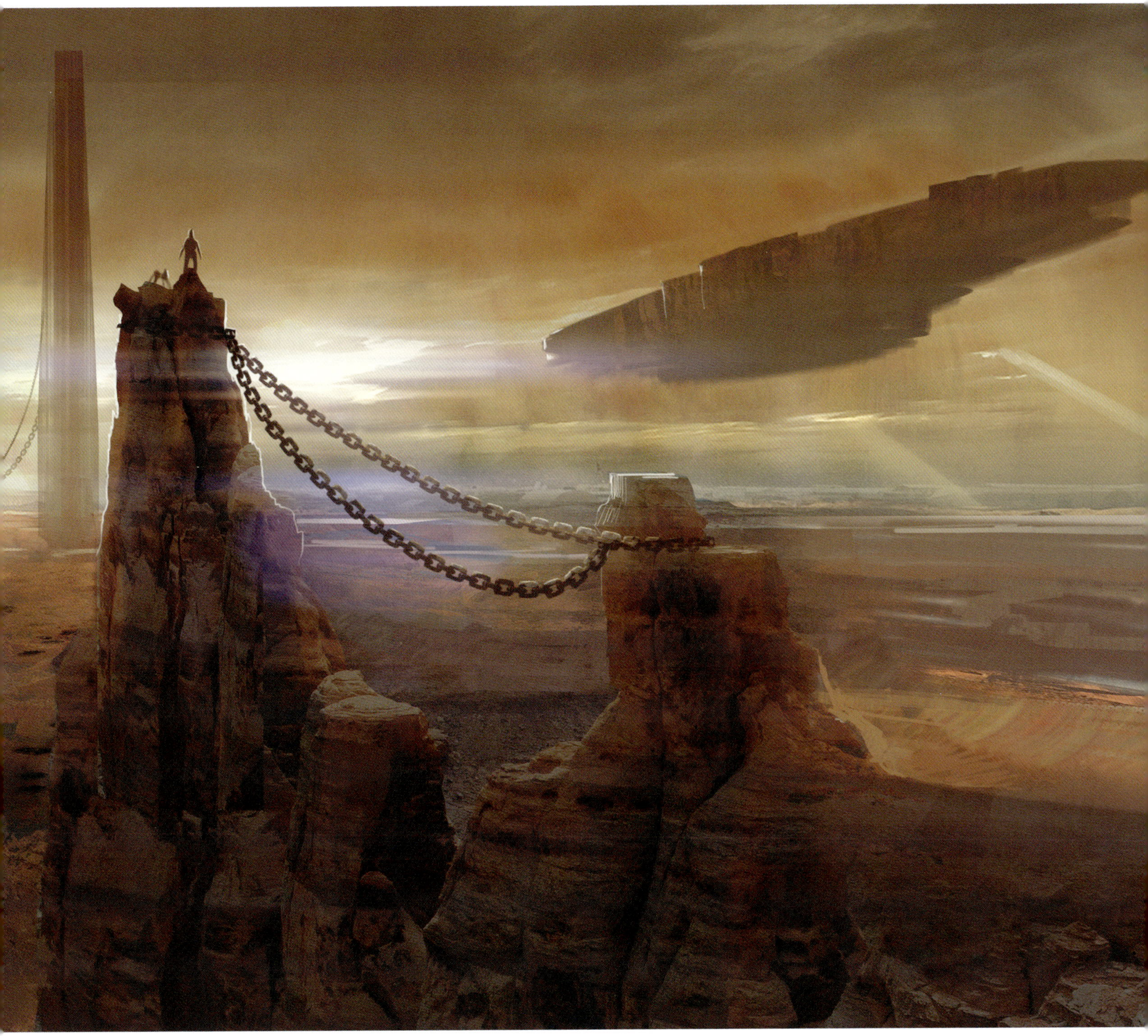

Thomas Pringle

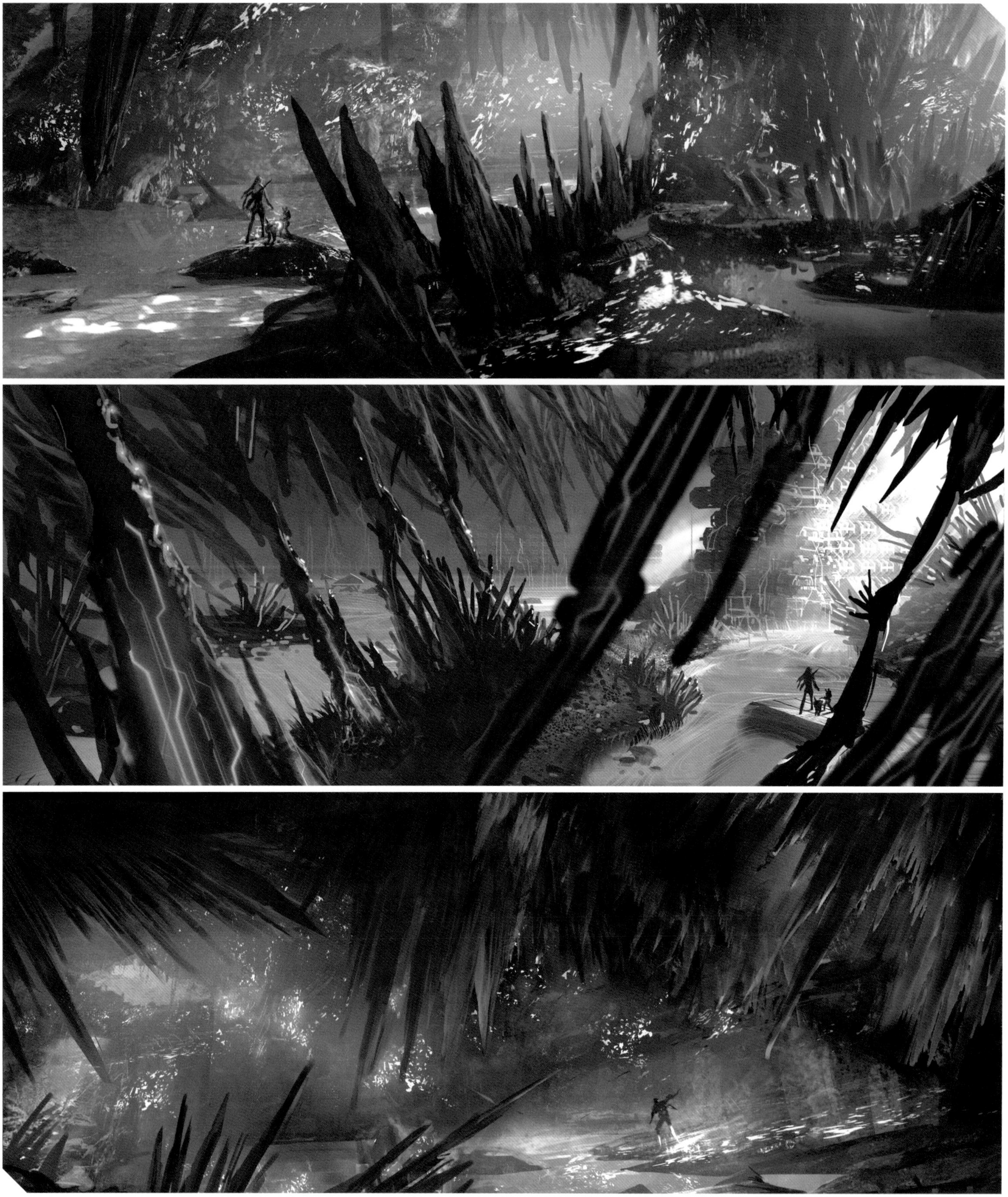

Todd Keller, Craig Sellars, and Patrice Bourroncle

In some explorations, the caves only featured the corrupt elements. This was unworkable, as without any contrasting elements players would have a much harder time navigating through the space.

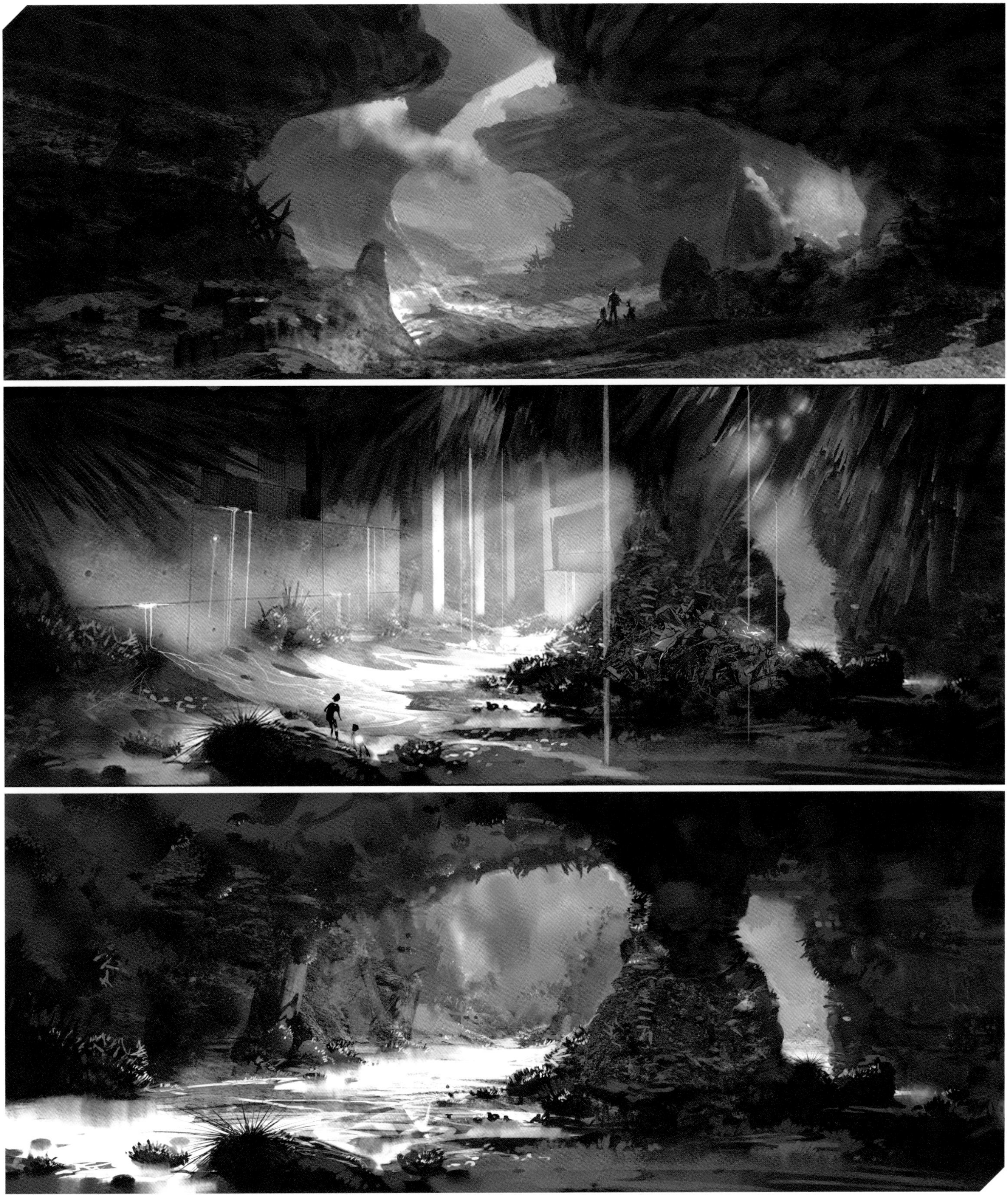

Todd Keller, Craig Sellars, and Patrice Bourroncle

Another consideration was how close the player could get to these corruption spikes; in some cases, the player could reach areas they were never intended to access, breaking game play.

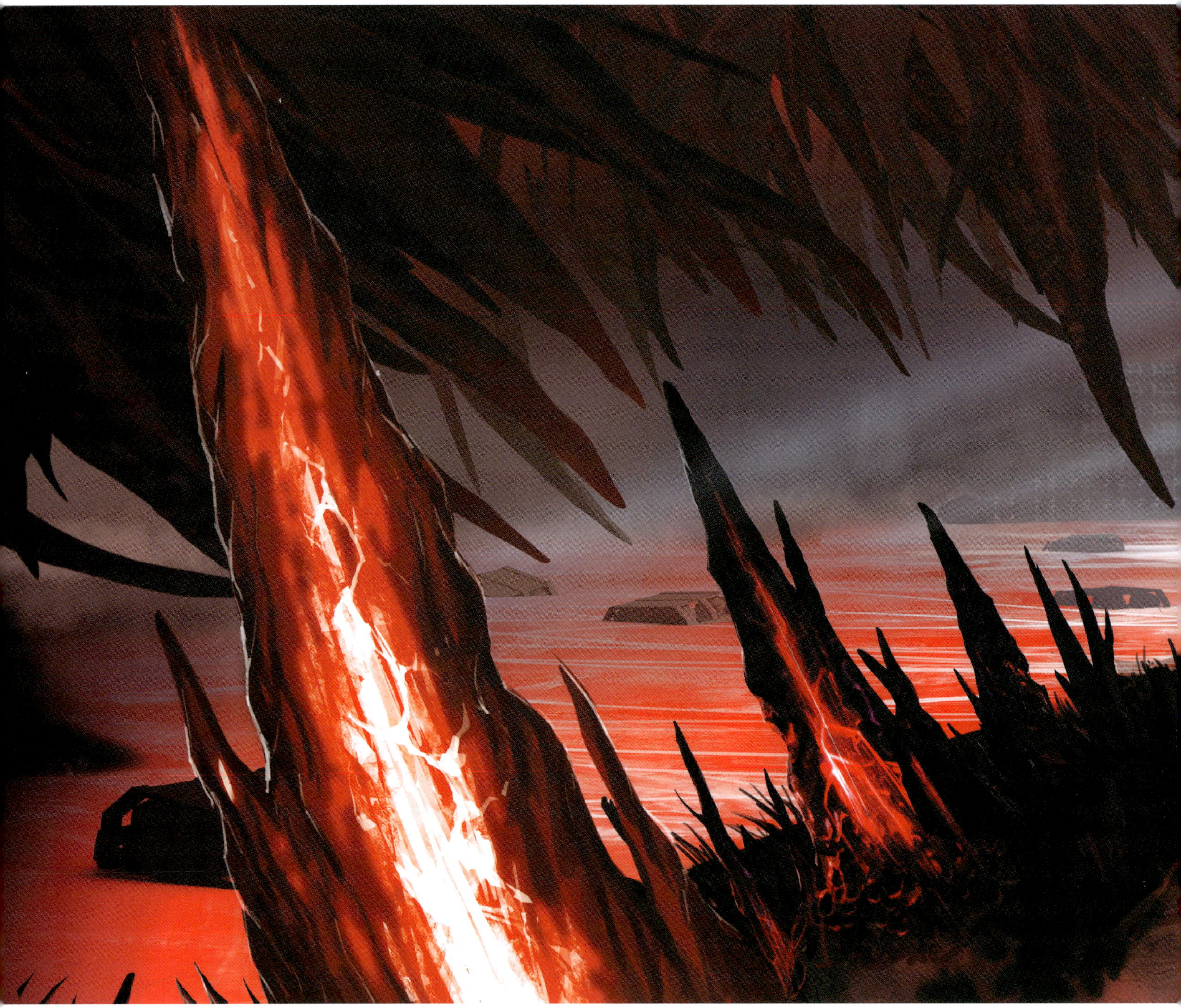

We also wanted to explore elements that pushed us away from a primarily rocky look for the corrupted caverns. Here a river of polluted E-Turner suggested a wetness that helped drive the in-game materials in a direction different from other game areas.

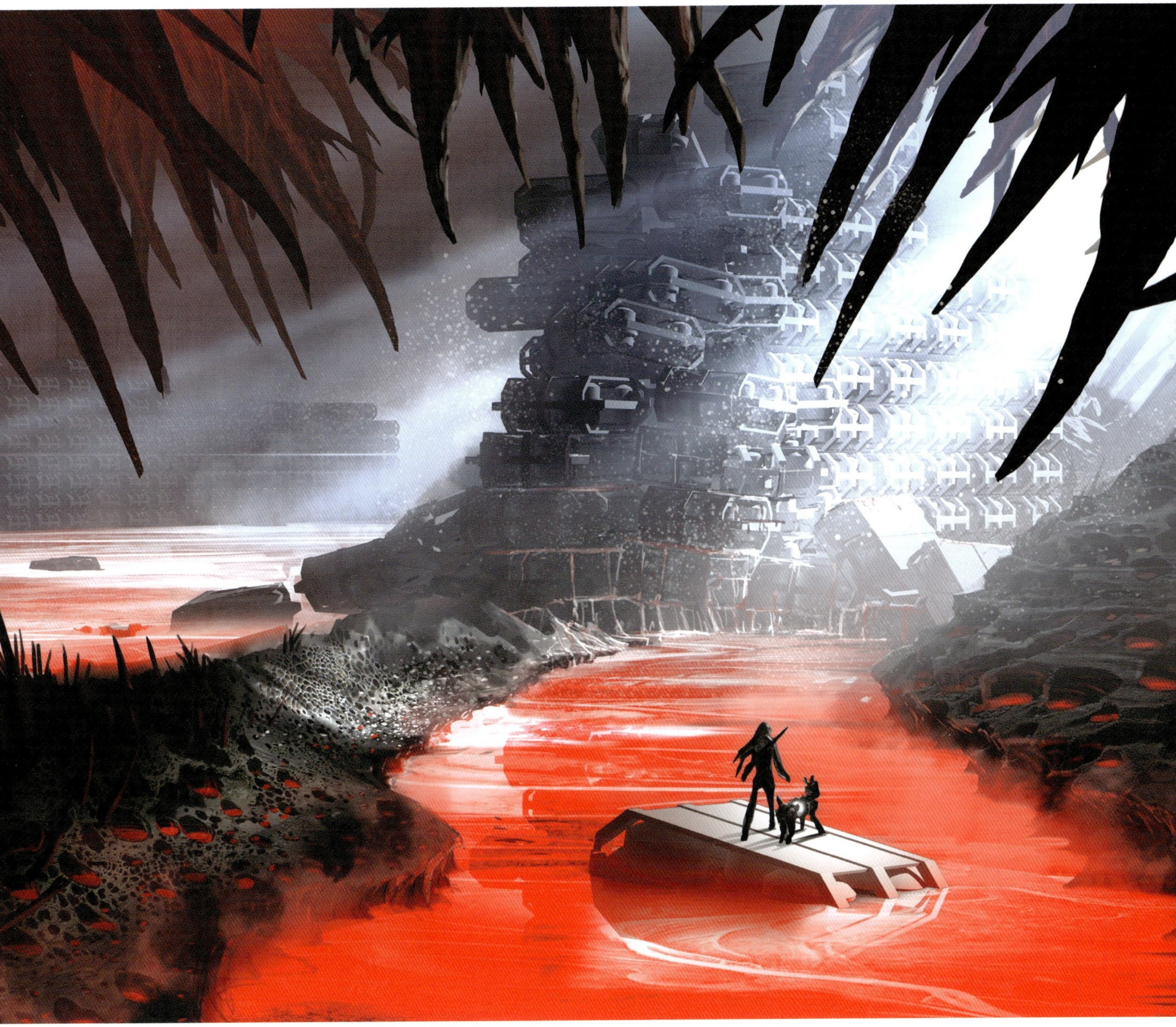

Damien Papet

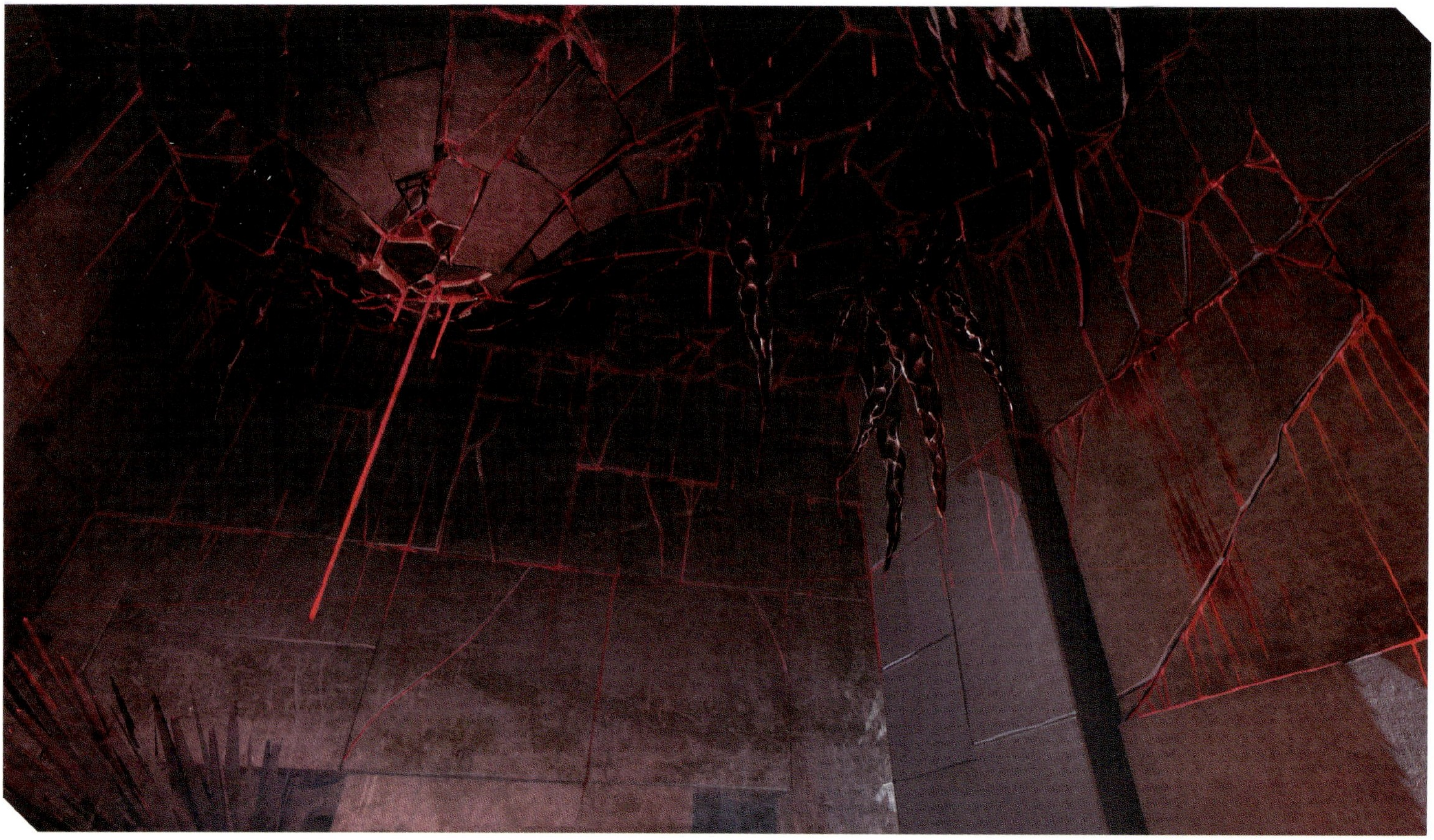

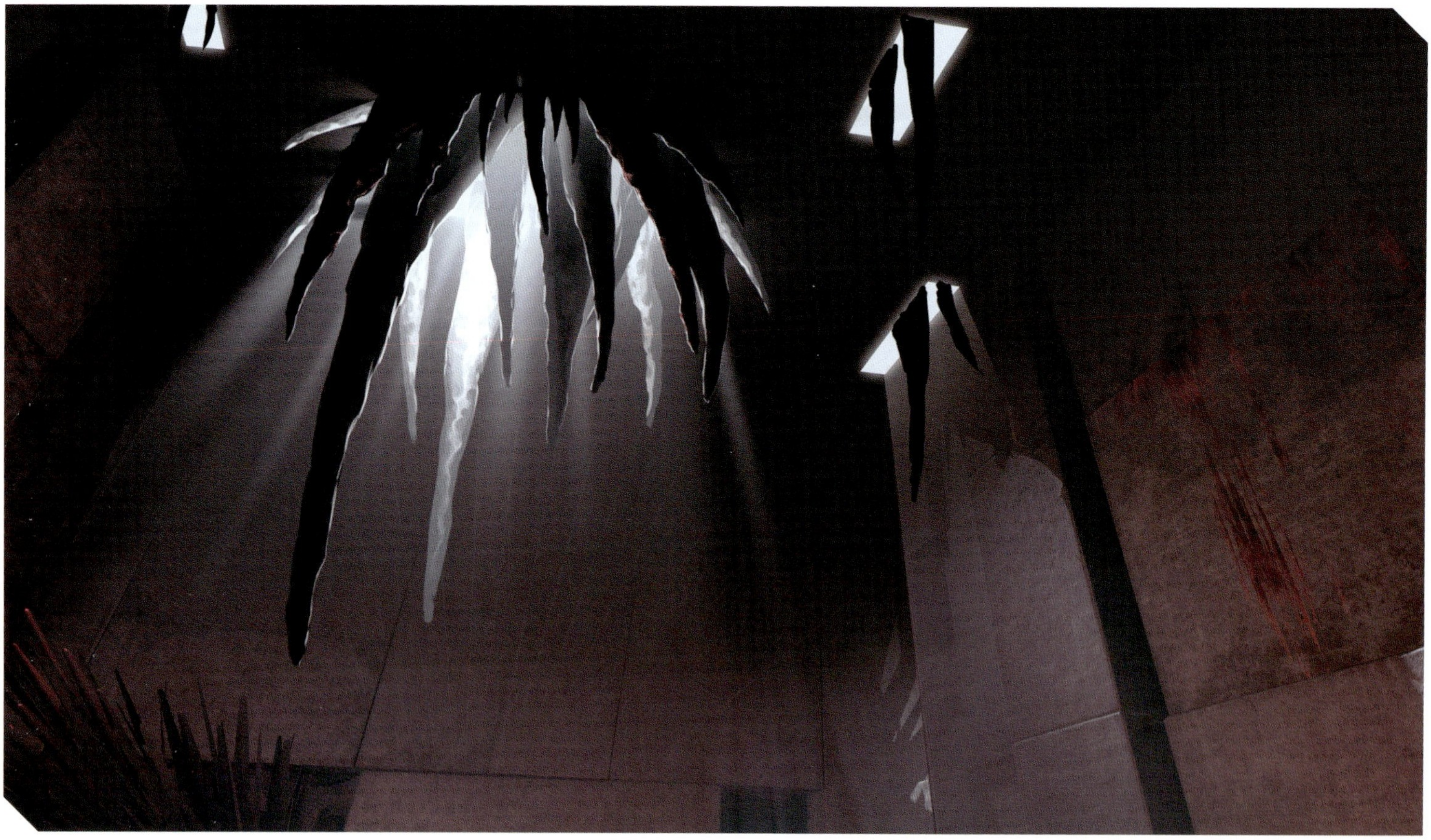

Damien Papet

Inside Far Eden Tower, above, Joule finally sees the extent of Victor's corruption. On the facing page, the security systems of the tower now answer to Victor and actively try to keep Joule from reaching the upper floors with laser barriers, movable platforms, and other hazards.

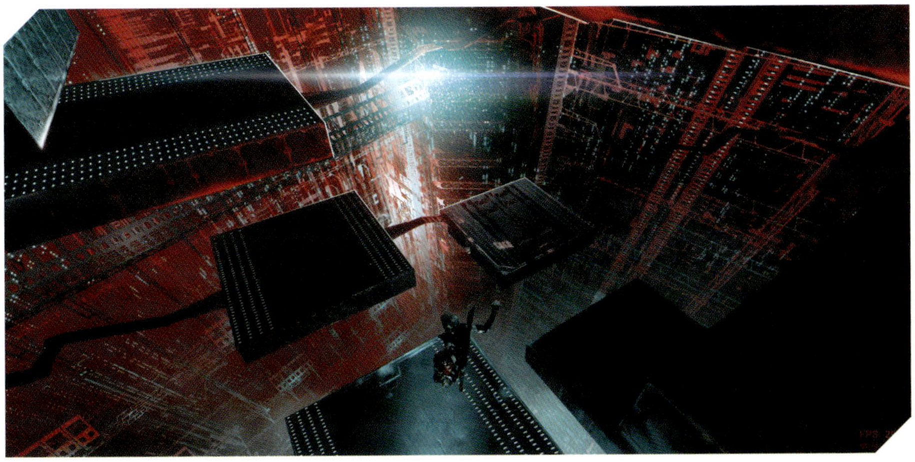

E-TOWER

Nothing on Far Eden matches the power and technology of the E-Tower. We wanted the interior to feel very foreign to what Joule has encountered so far. However, even in the E-Tower, evidence of Victor's corruption is visible.

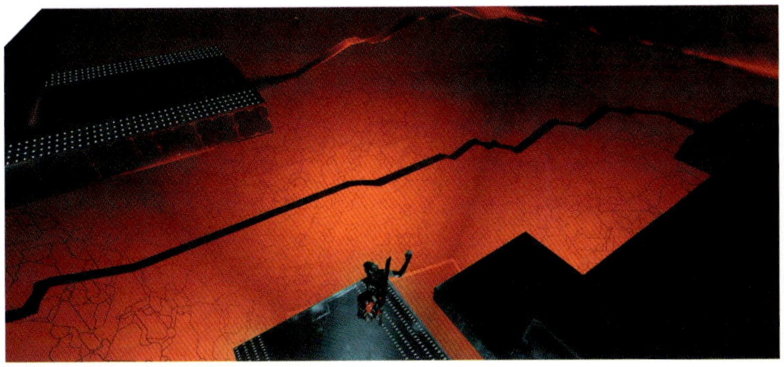

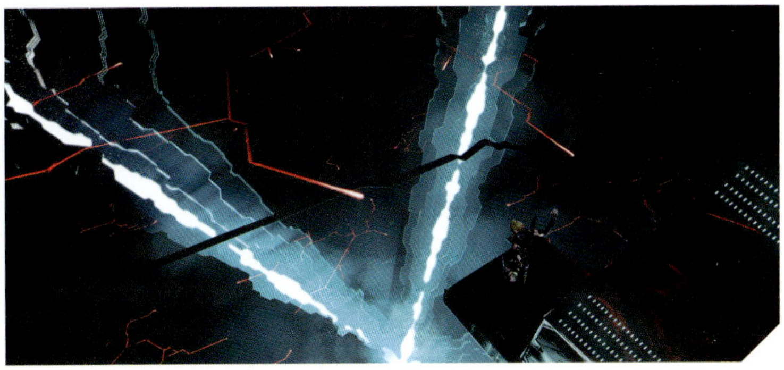

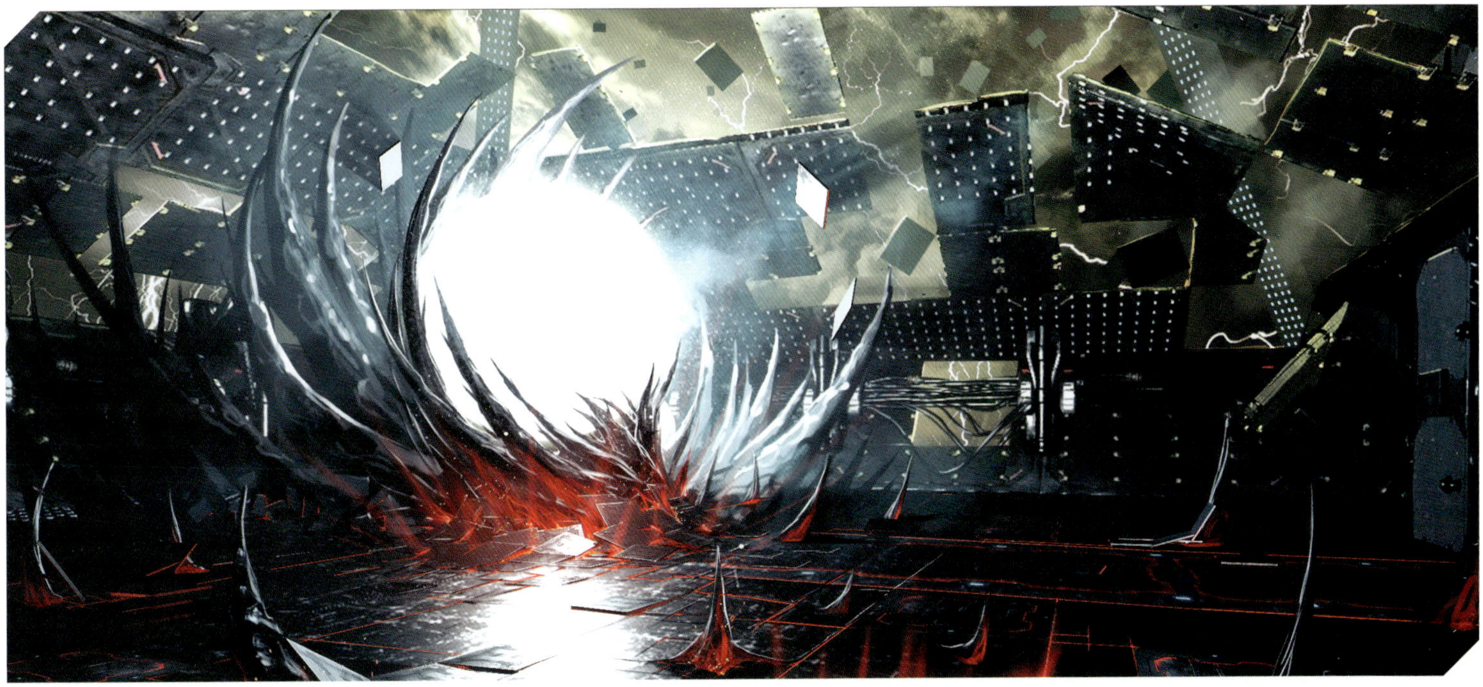

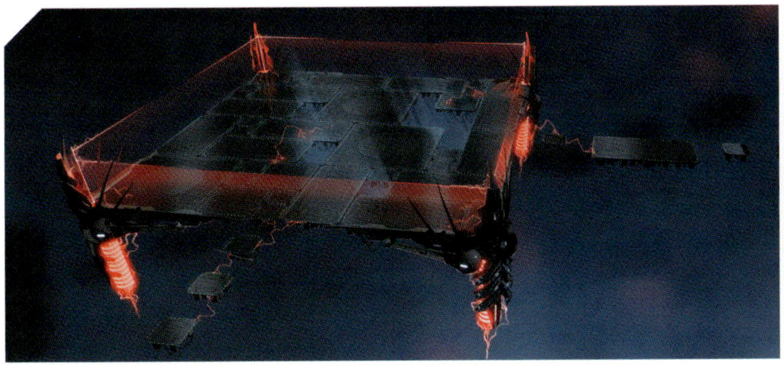

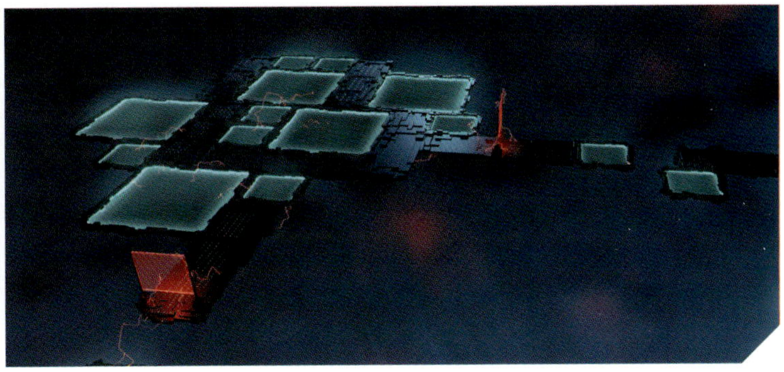

Todd Keller, Elizabeth Foster, and Damien Pupet

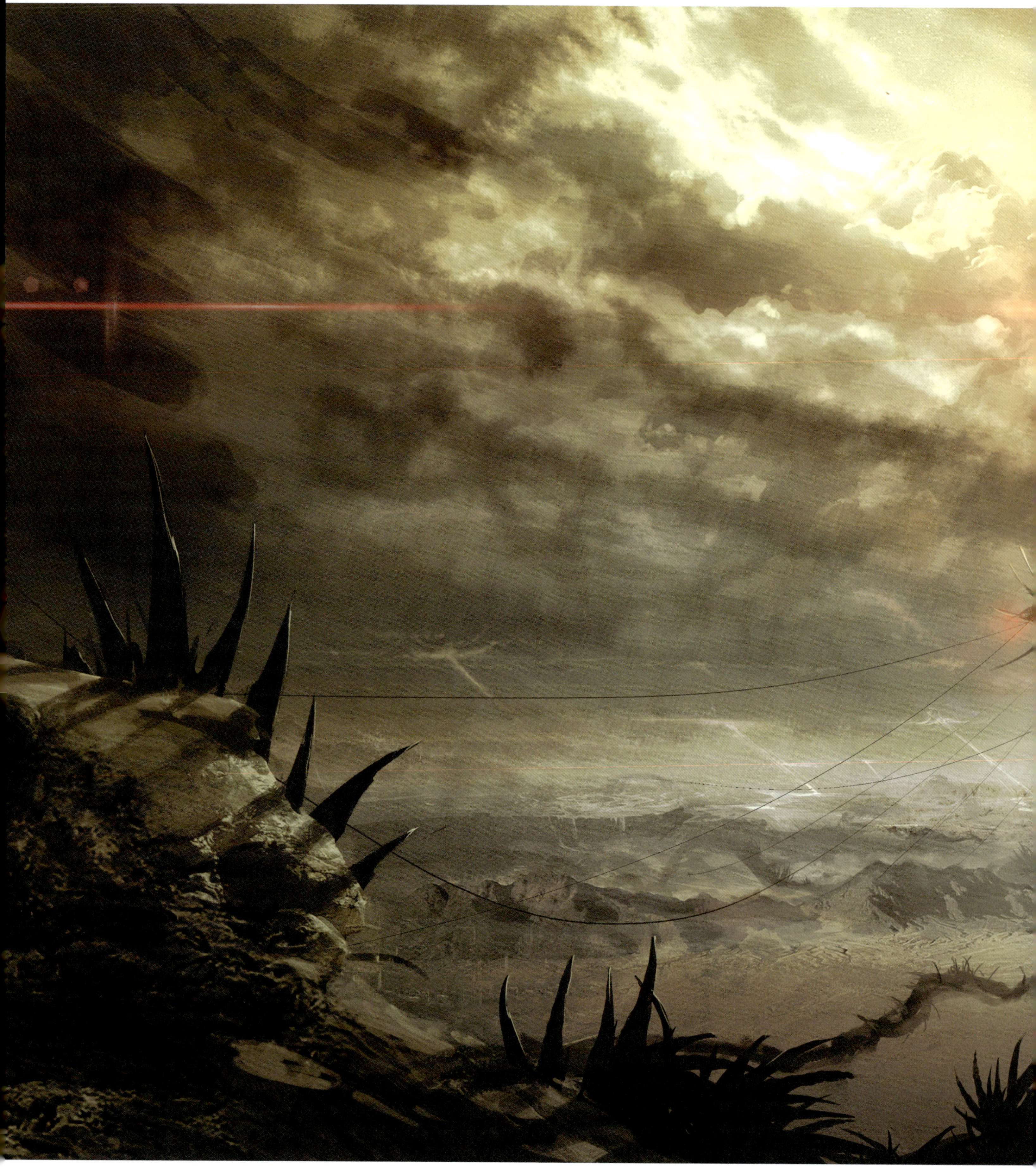

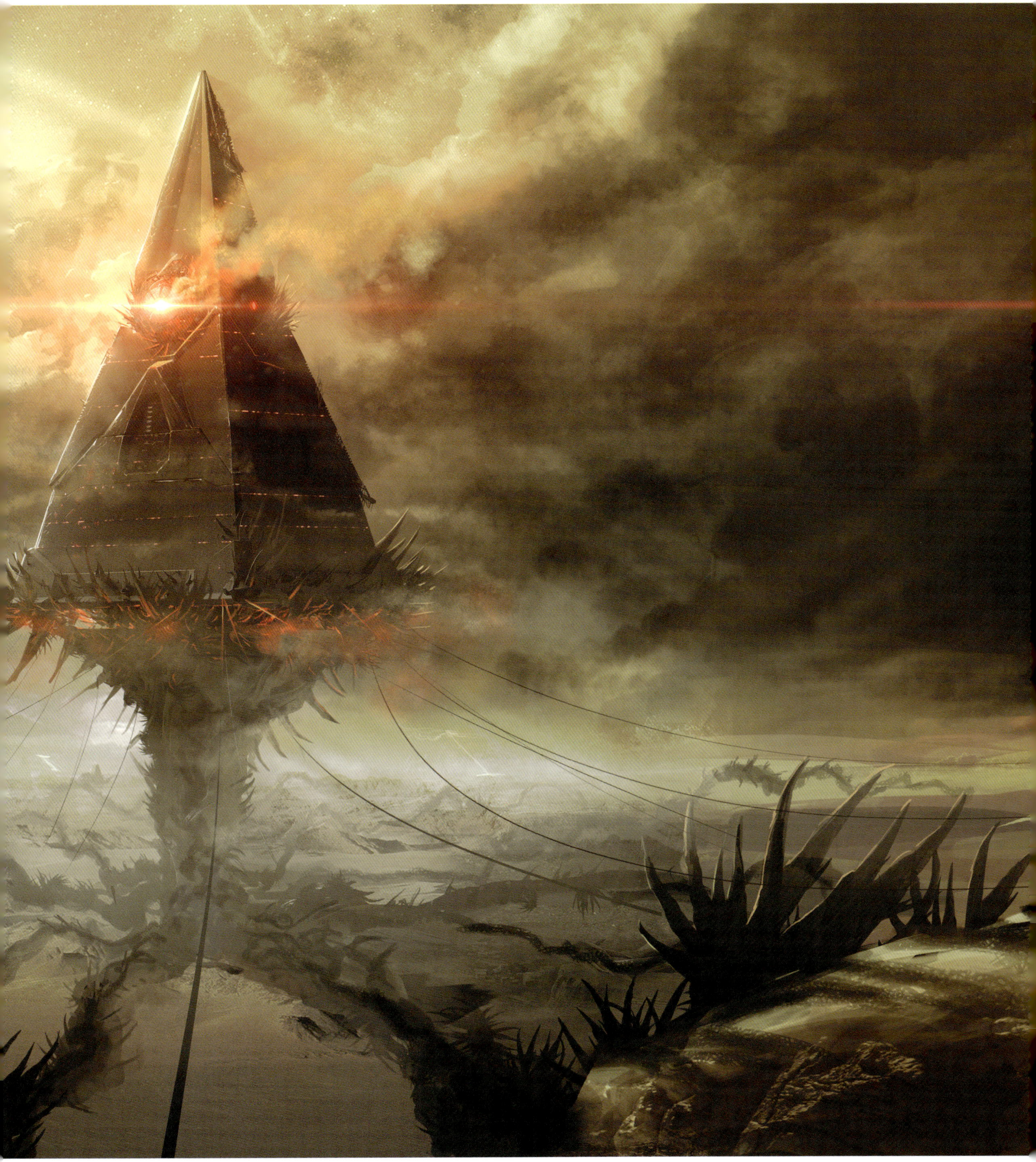

Damien Papet

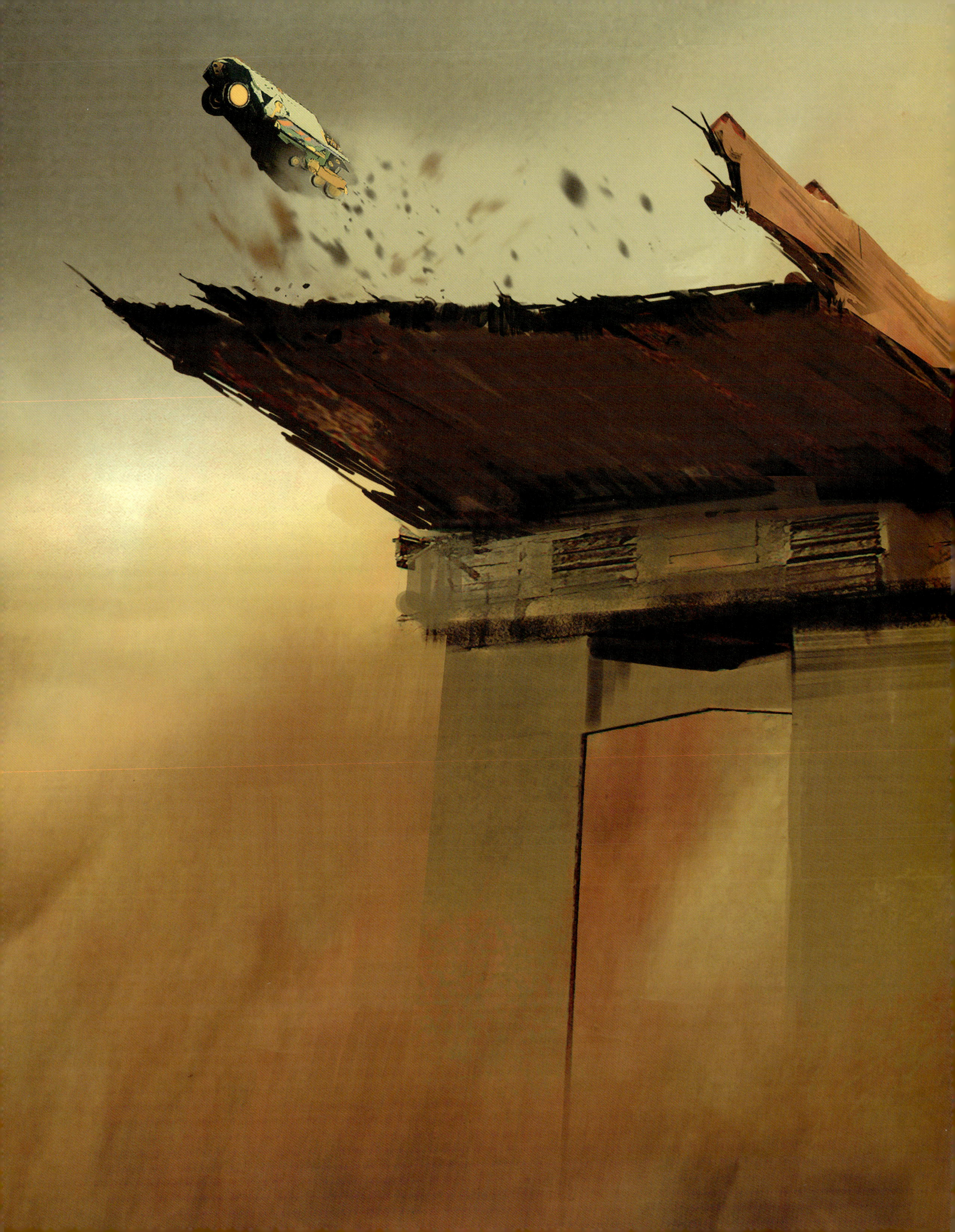

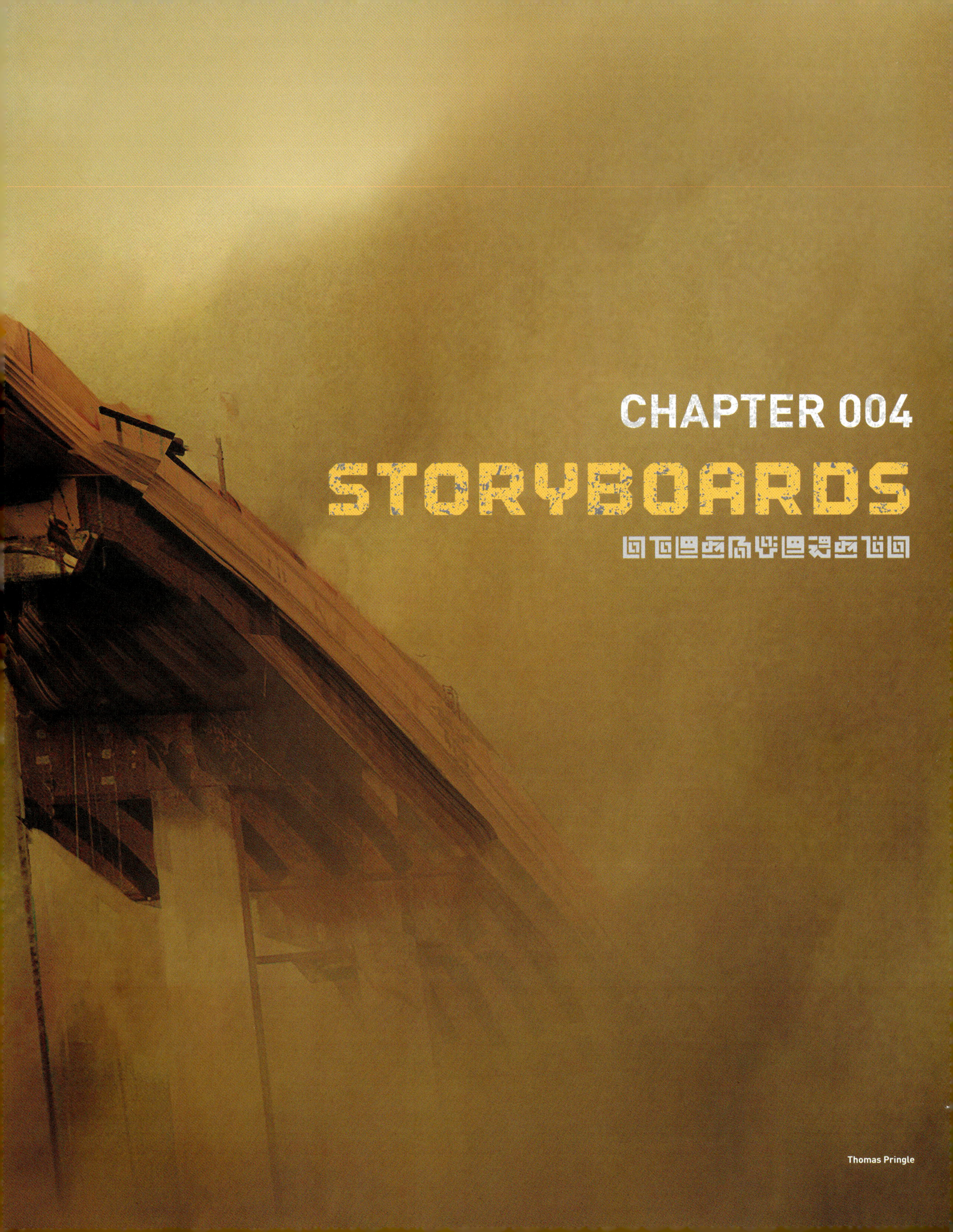

CHAPTER 004
STORYBOARDS

Thomas Pringle

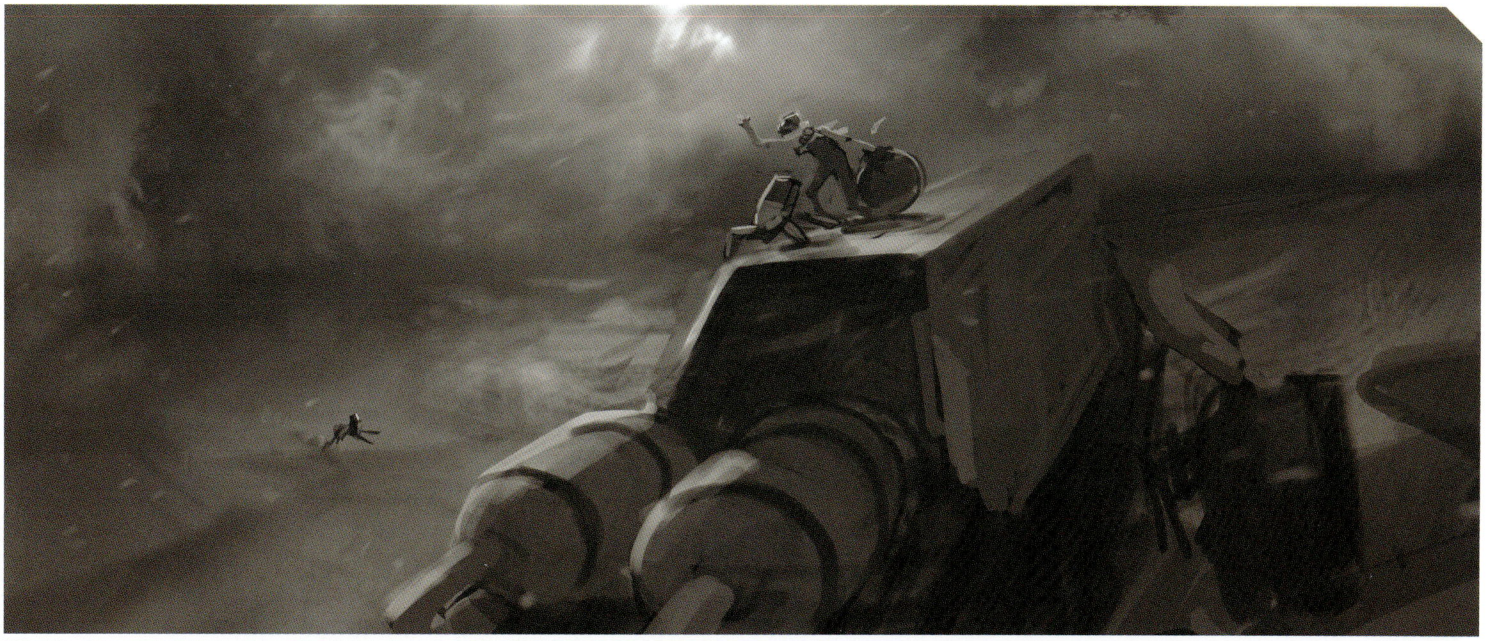

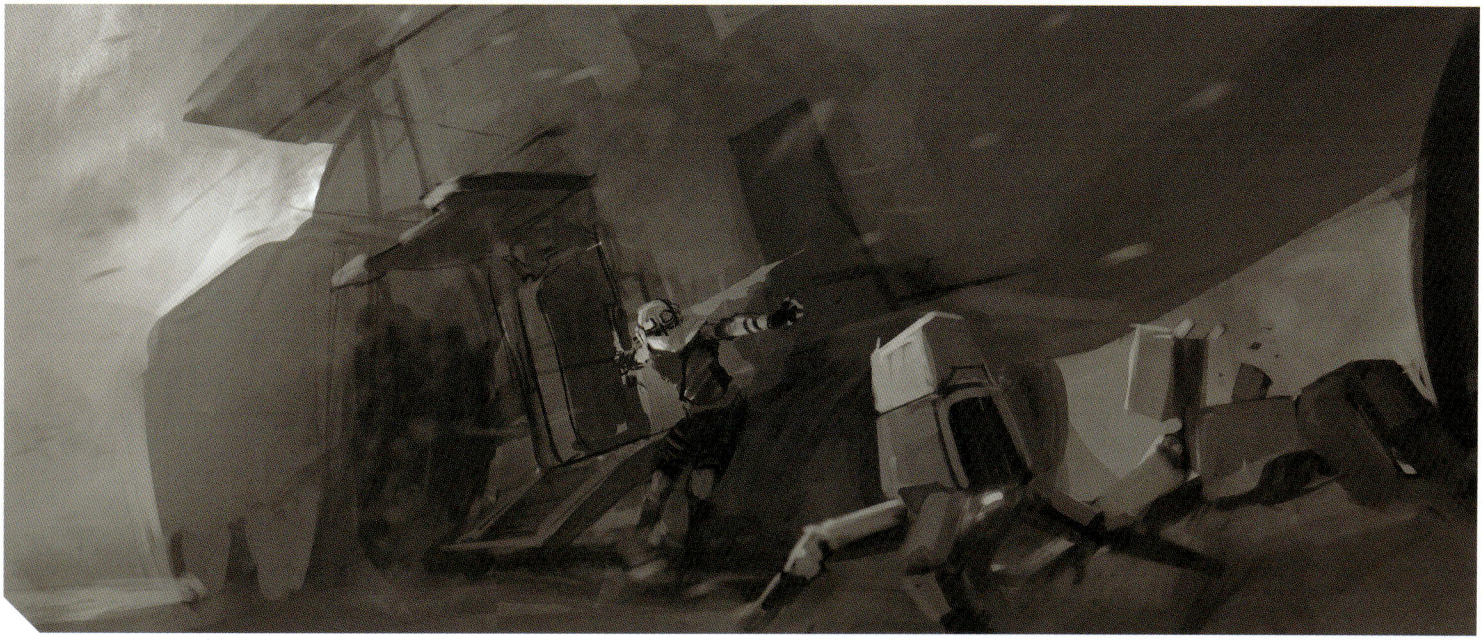

NARRATIVE BEATS

Storyboards from a proof-of-concept animatic show Joule and two of her Corebots, Mack and Seth, barely reaching her Crawler before it is engulfed by a violent sandstorm. Inside, she repairs an abandoned AP-3 frame. Parts of this early concept film evolved into a cinematic toward the end of the game where Joule discovers the last of three primary Cores, the red Core named Duncan.

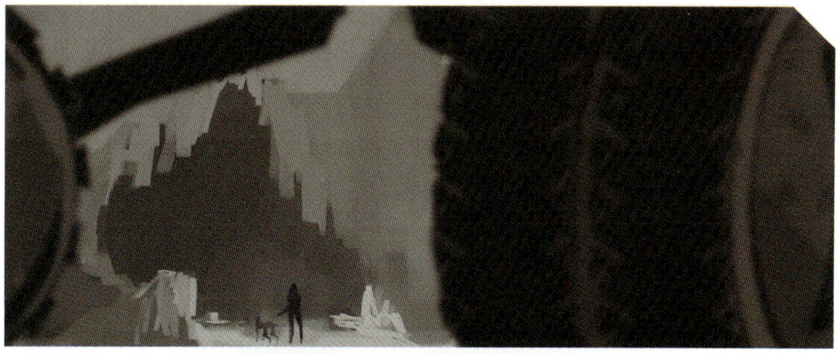

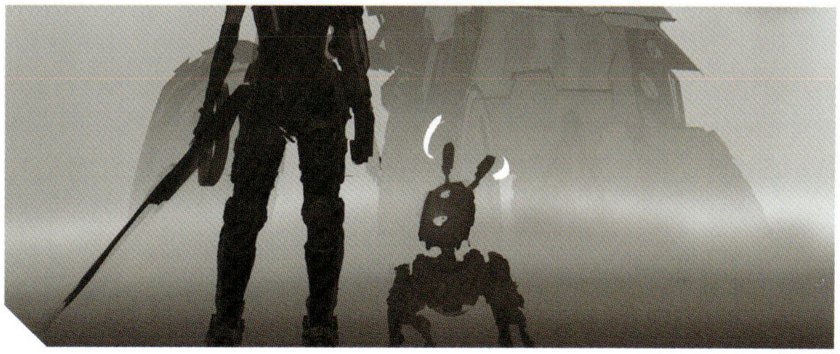

Craig Sellars and Hovic Alahaidoyan

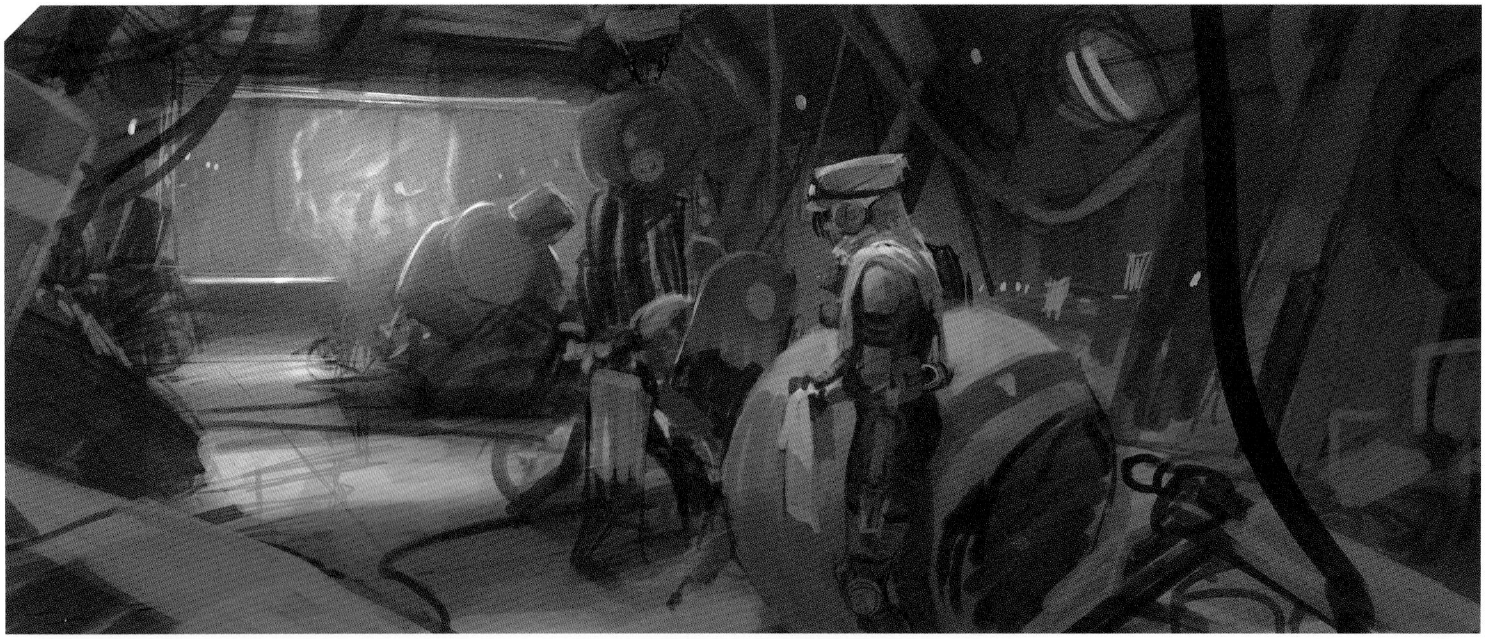

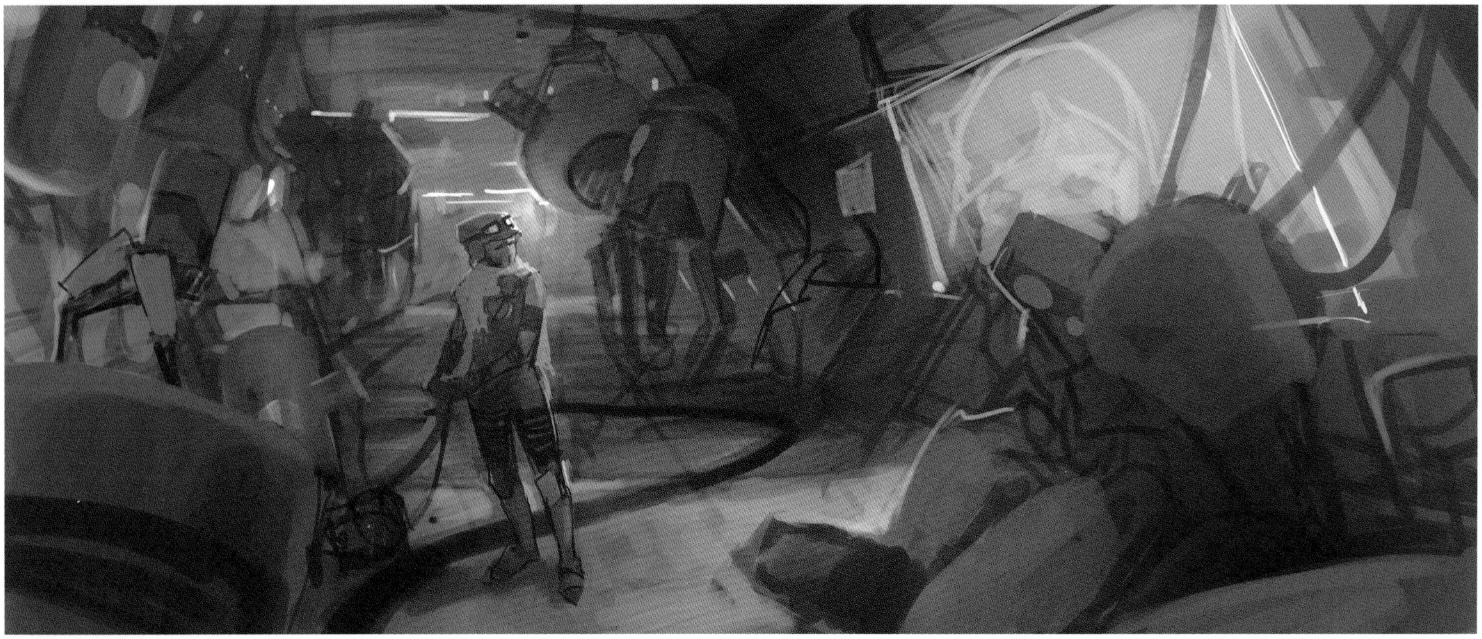

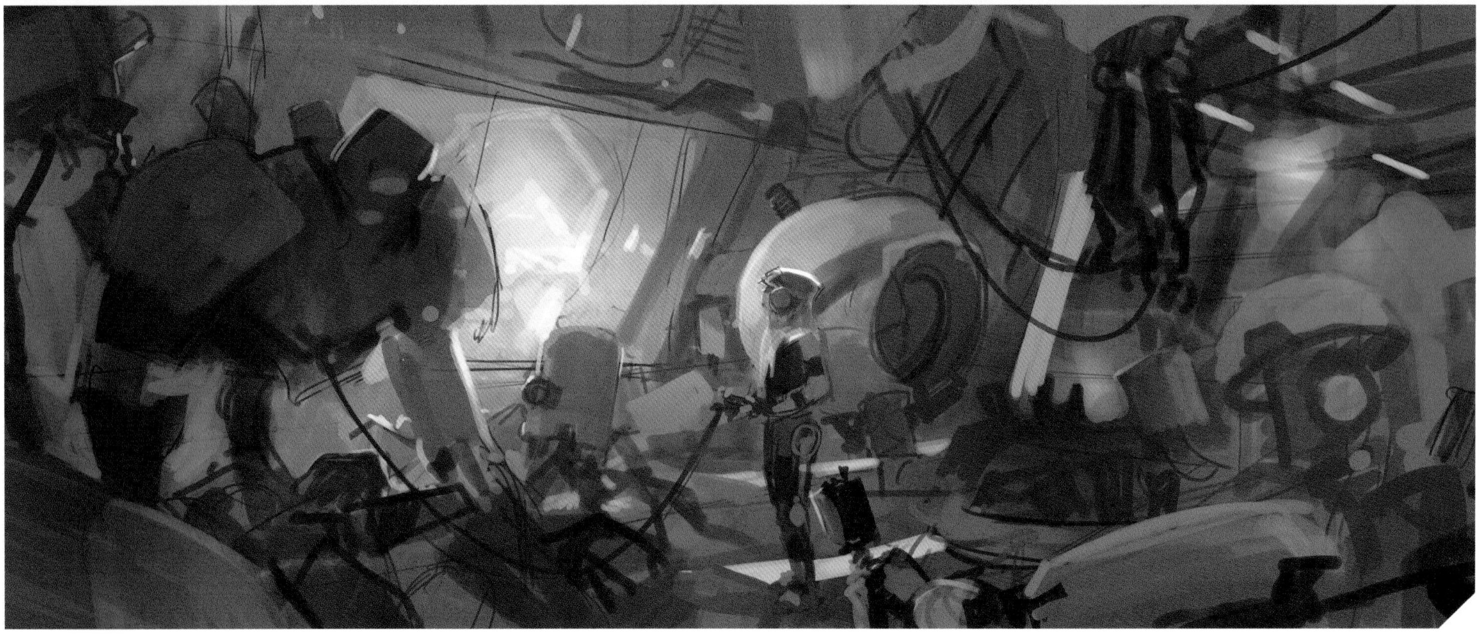

Craig Sellars and Hovic Alahaidoyan

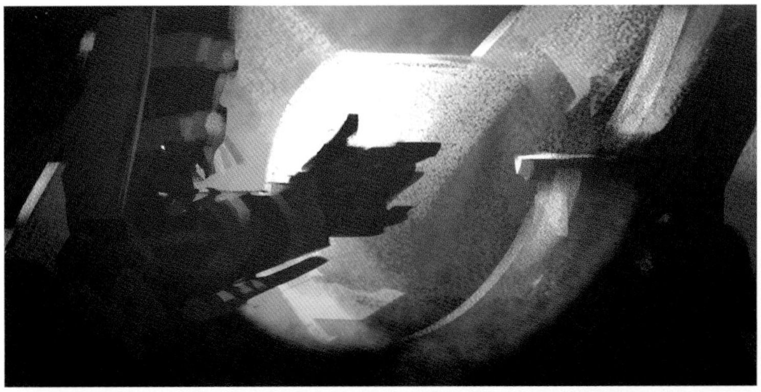

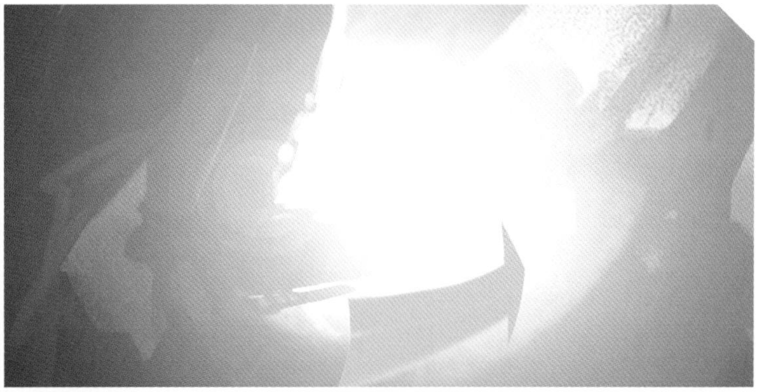

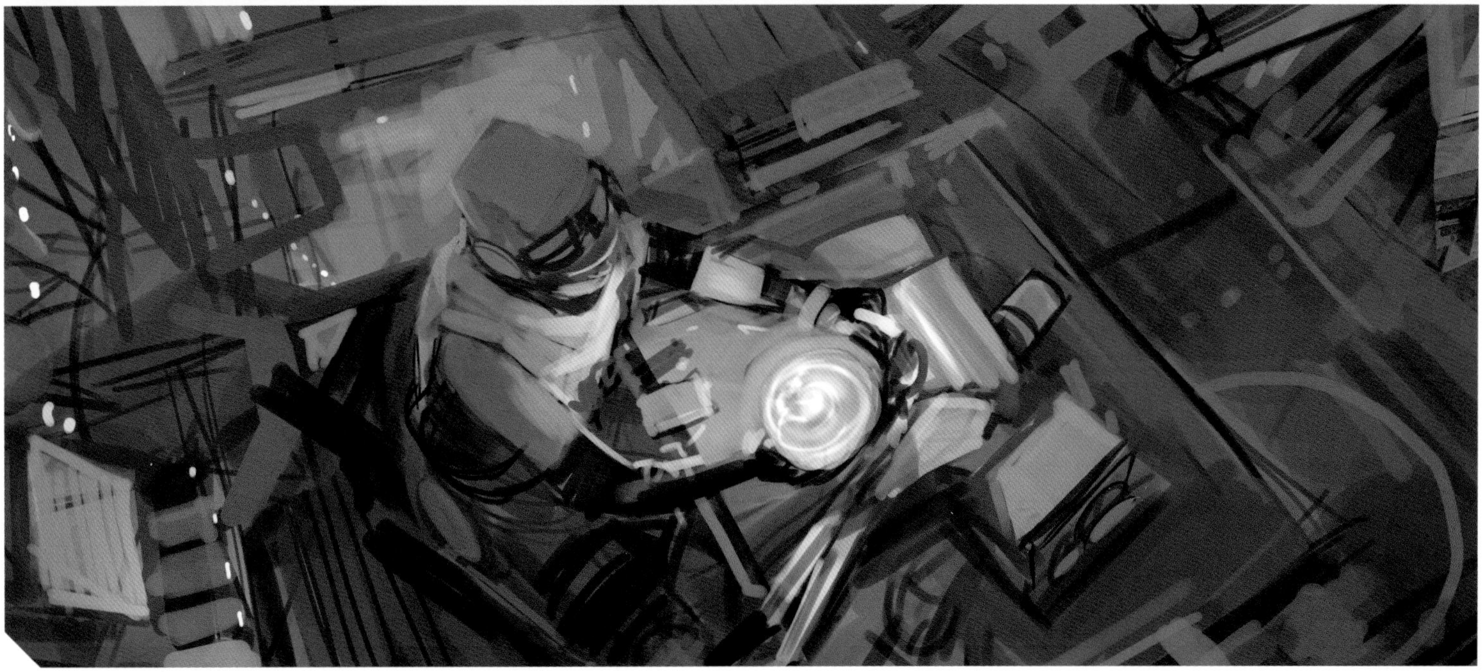

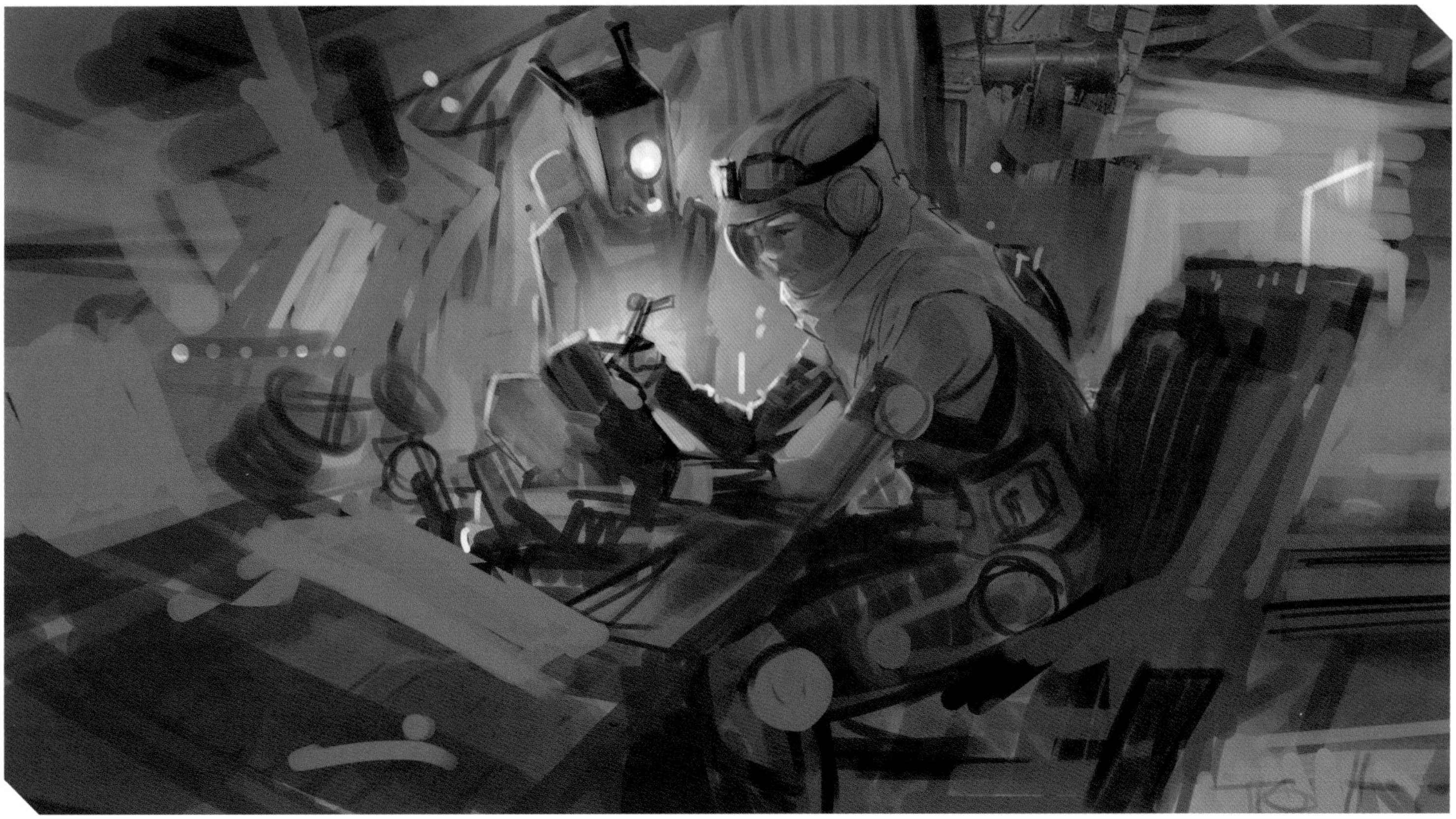

Craig Sellars and Hovic Alahaidoyan

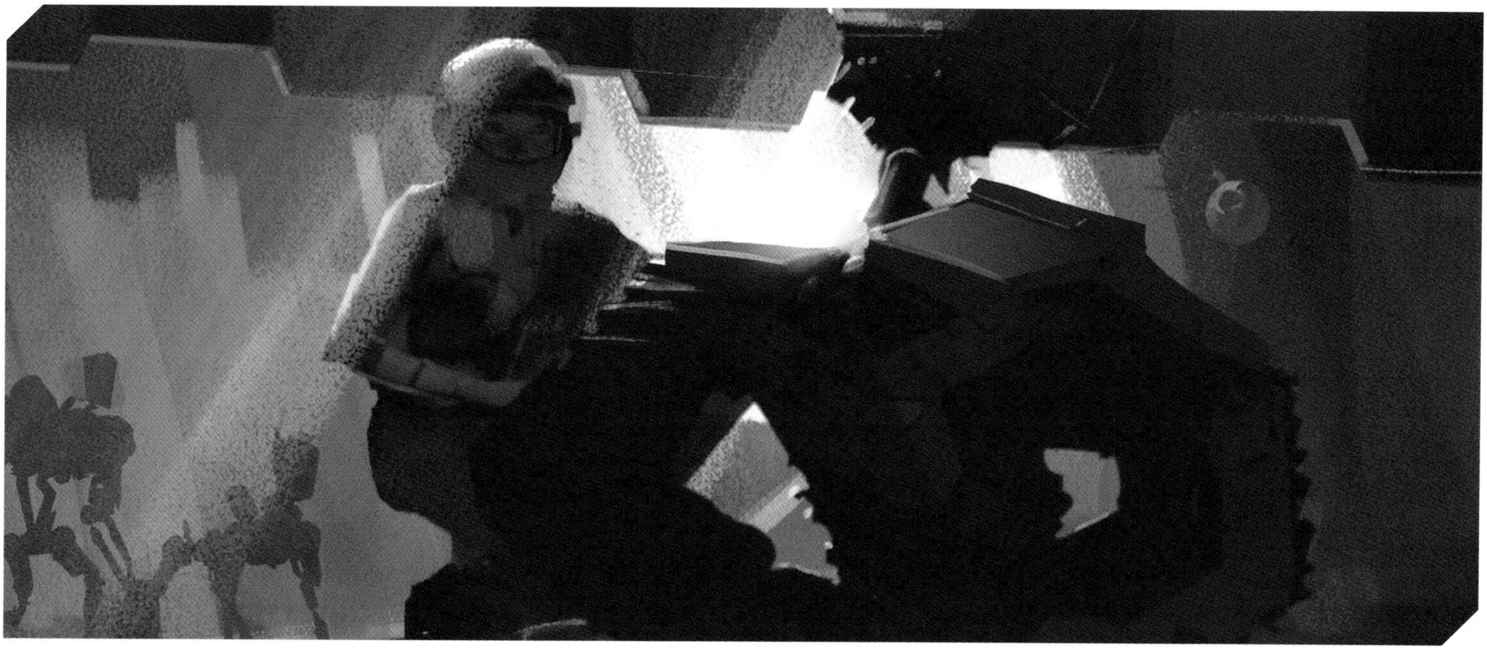

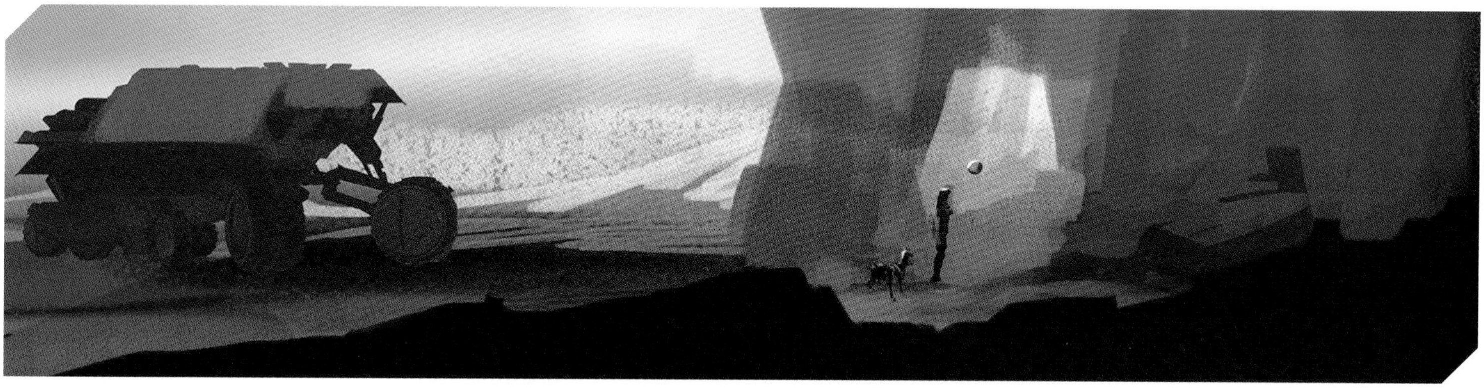

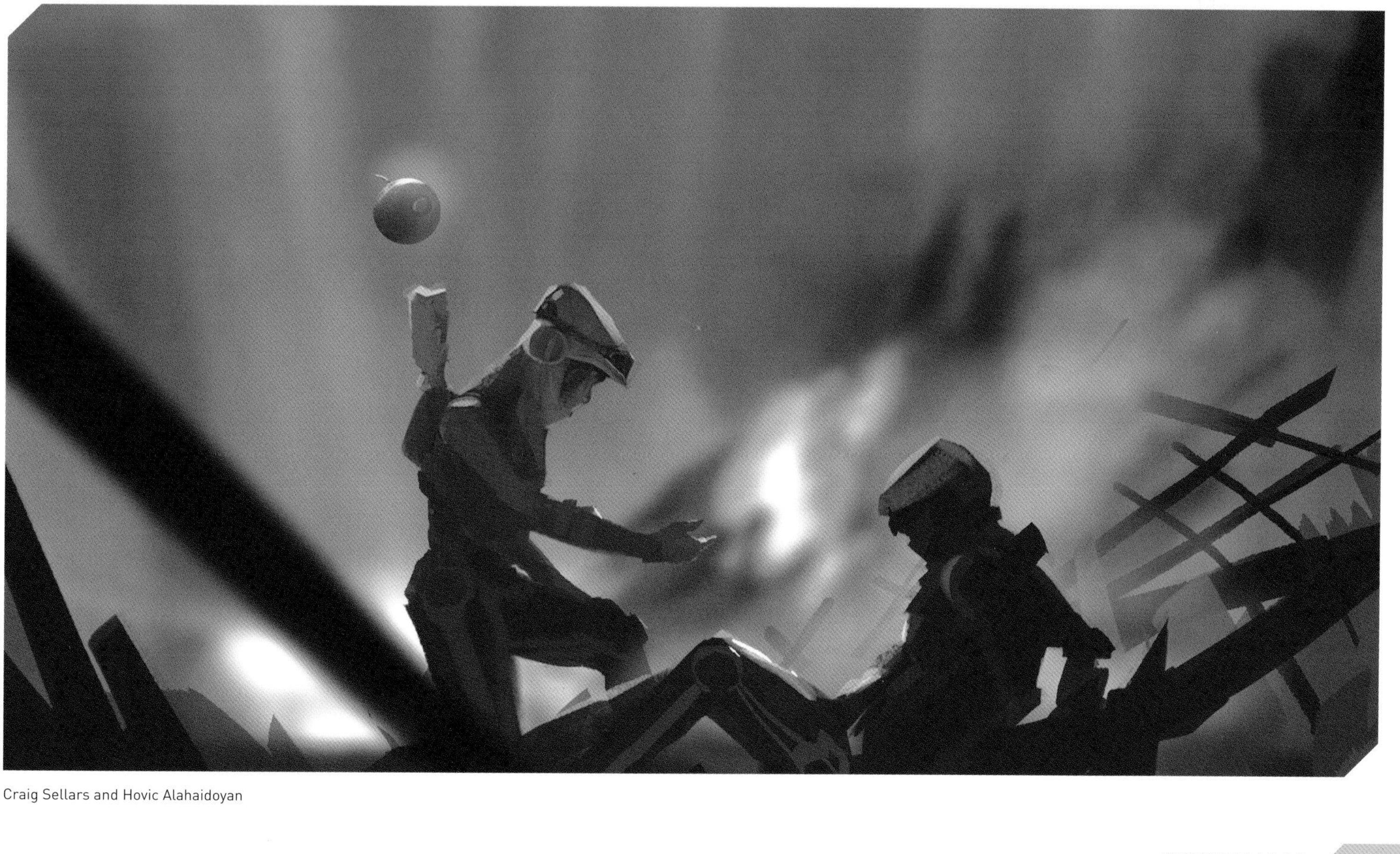

Craig Sellars and Hovic Alahaidoyan

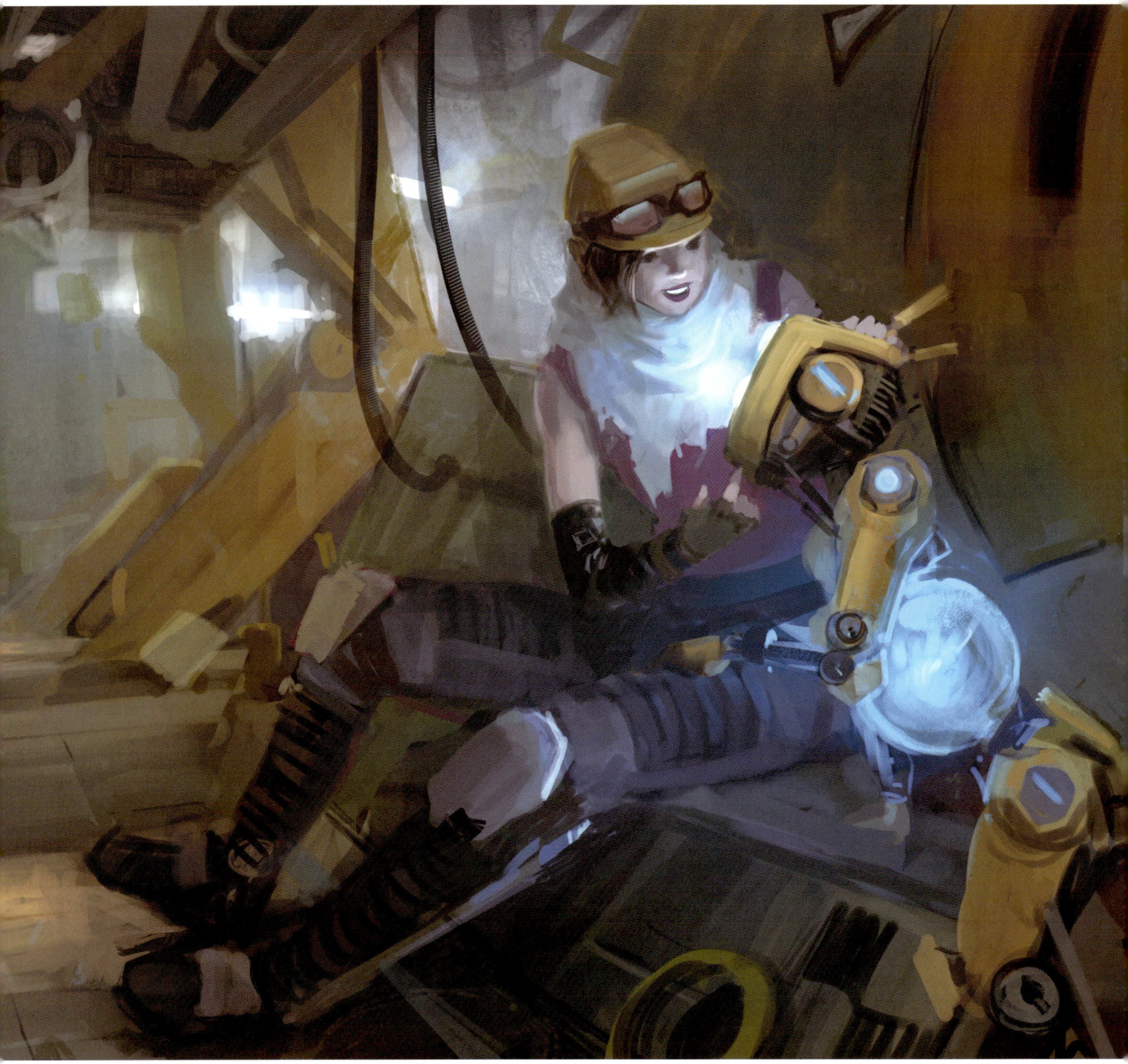

Mood boards like this one helped the team rally around the emotion of the story as well as the artistic style used to portray it.

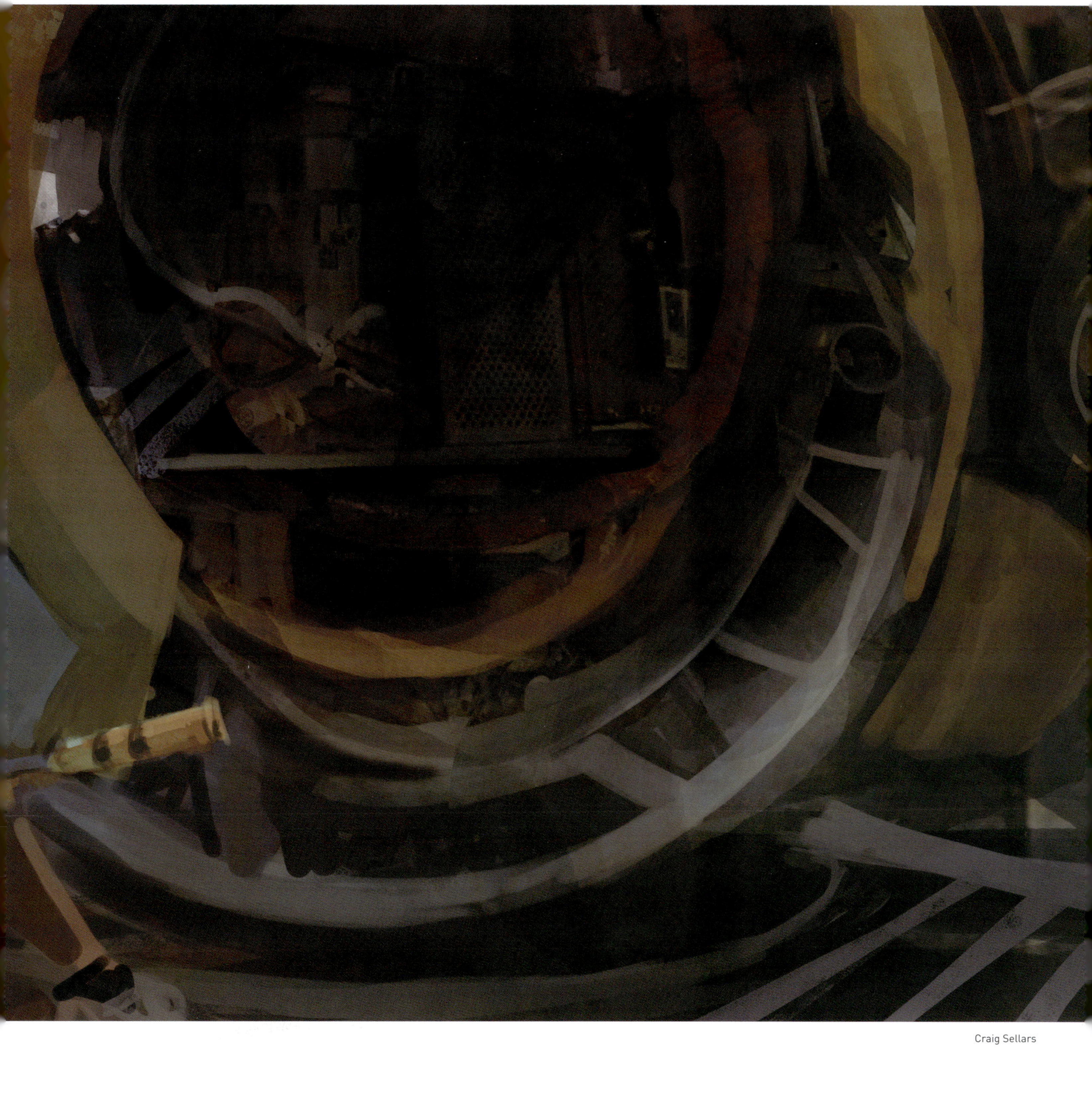

Craig Sellars

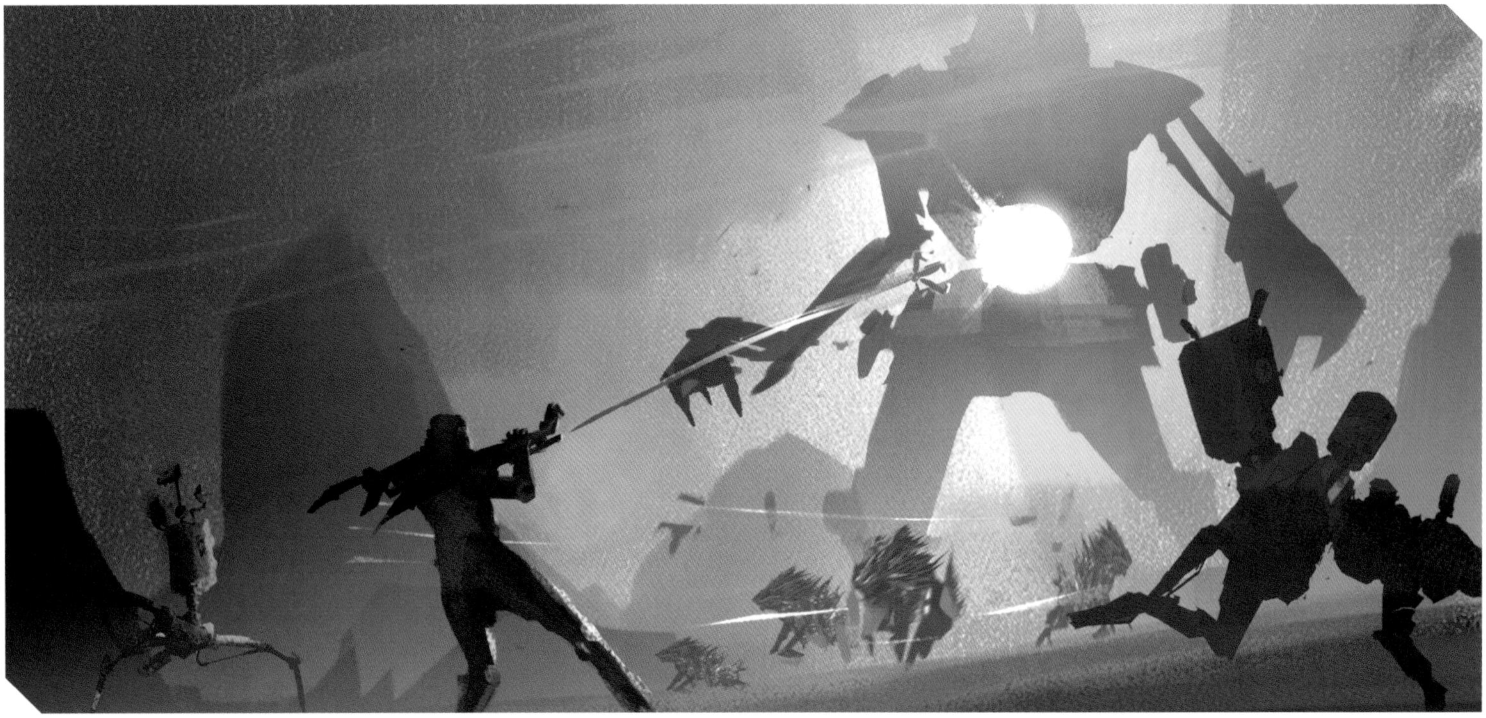

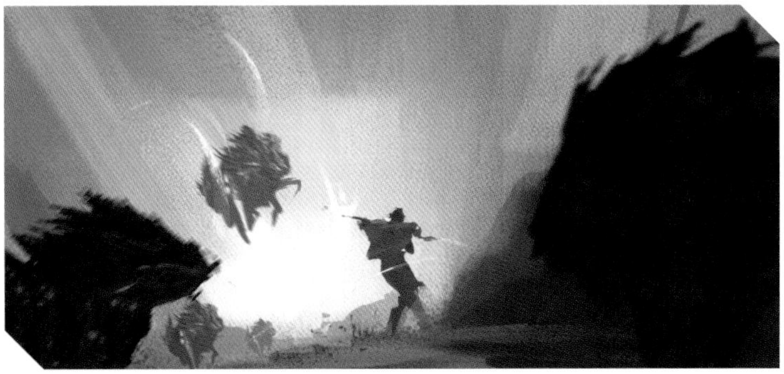

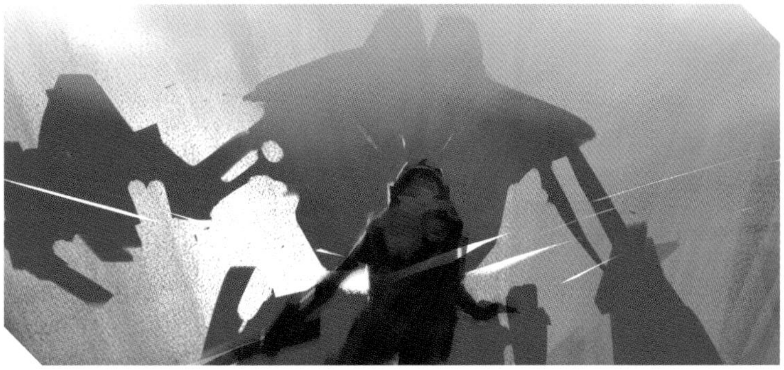

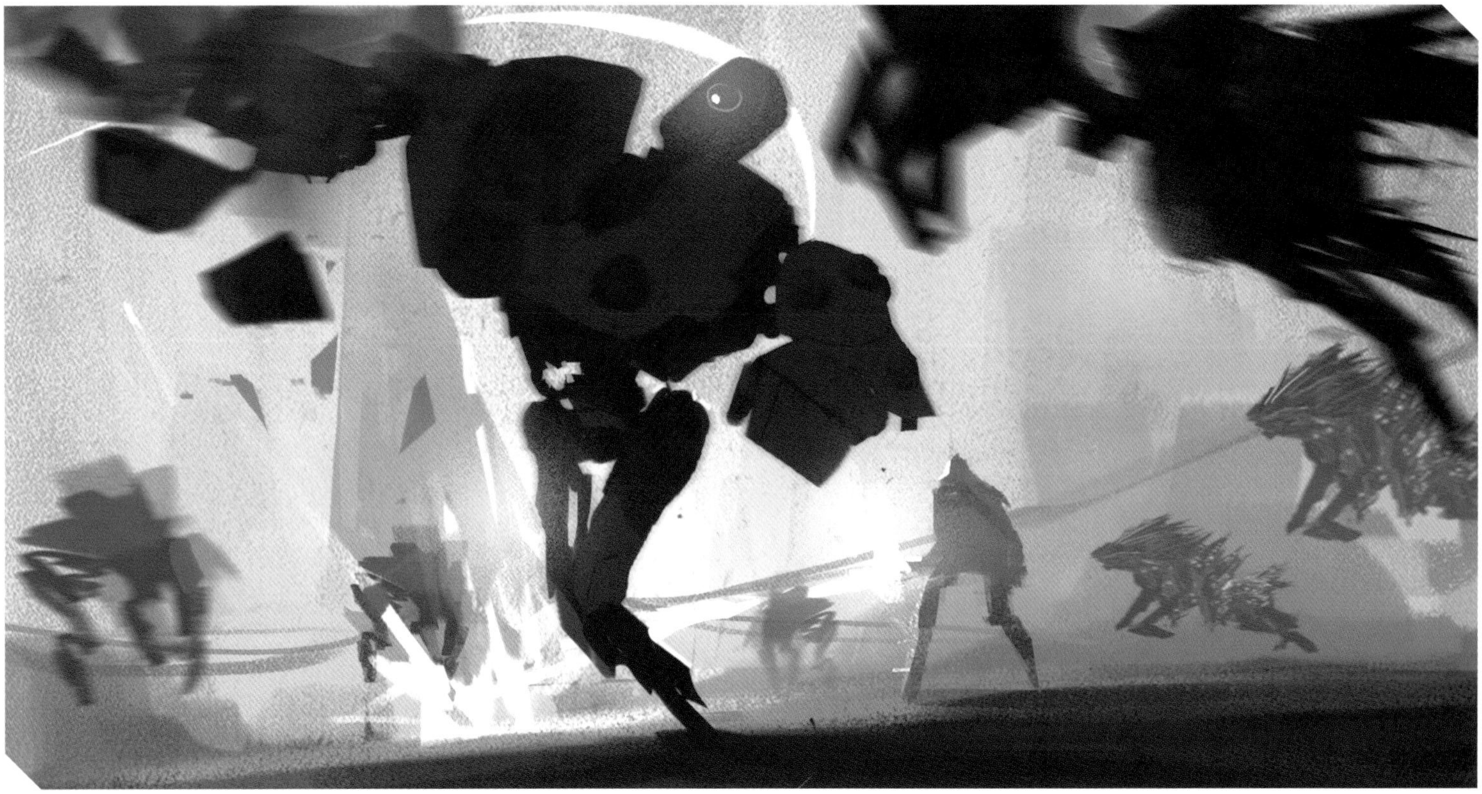

Hovic Alahaidoyan

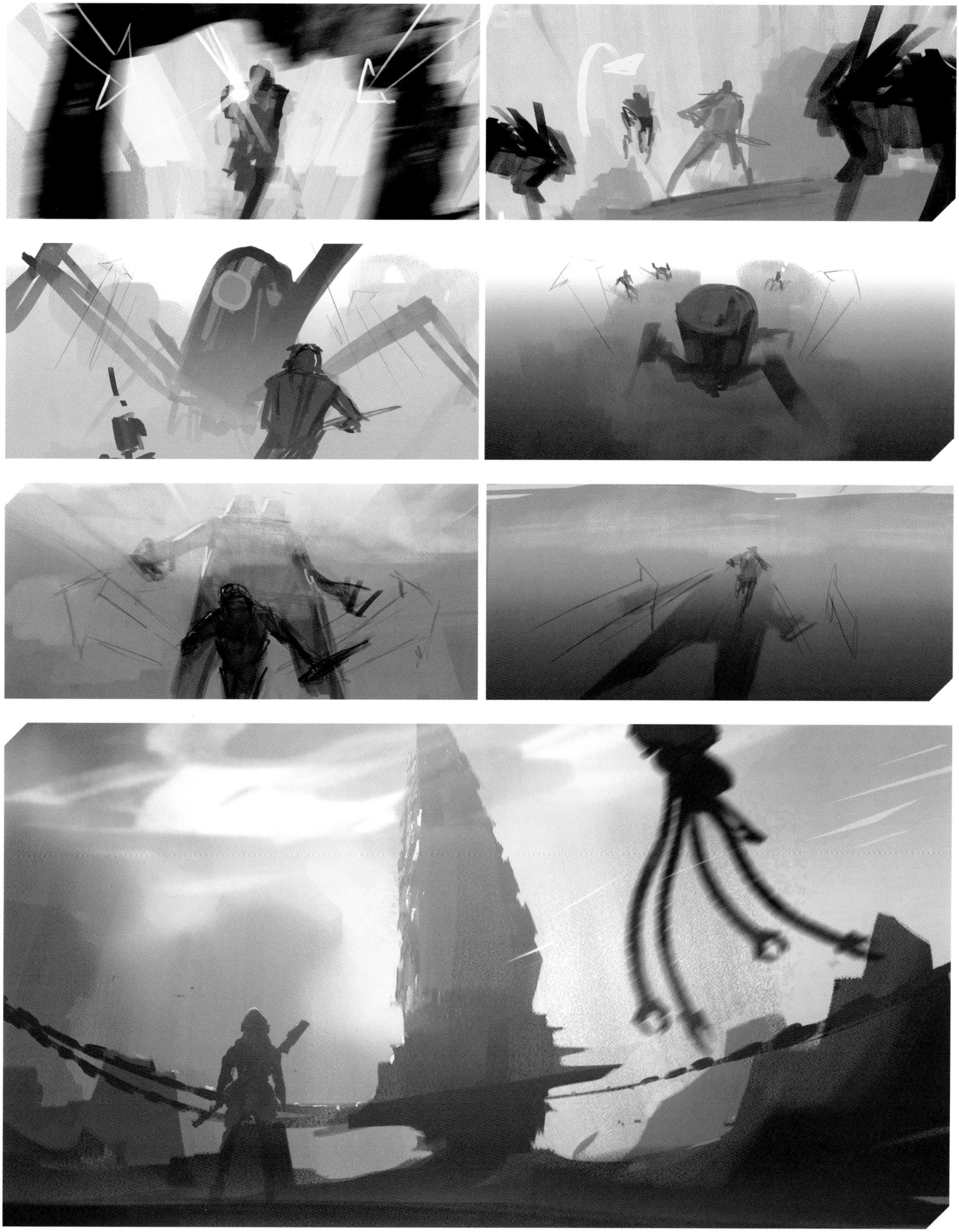

Hovic Alahaidoyan

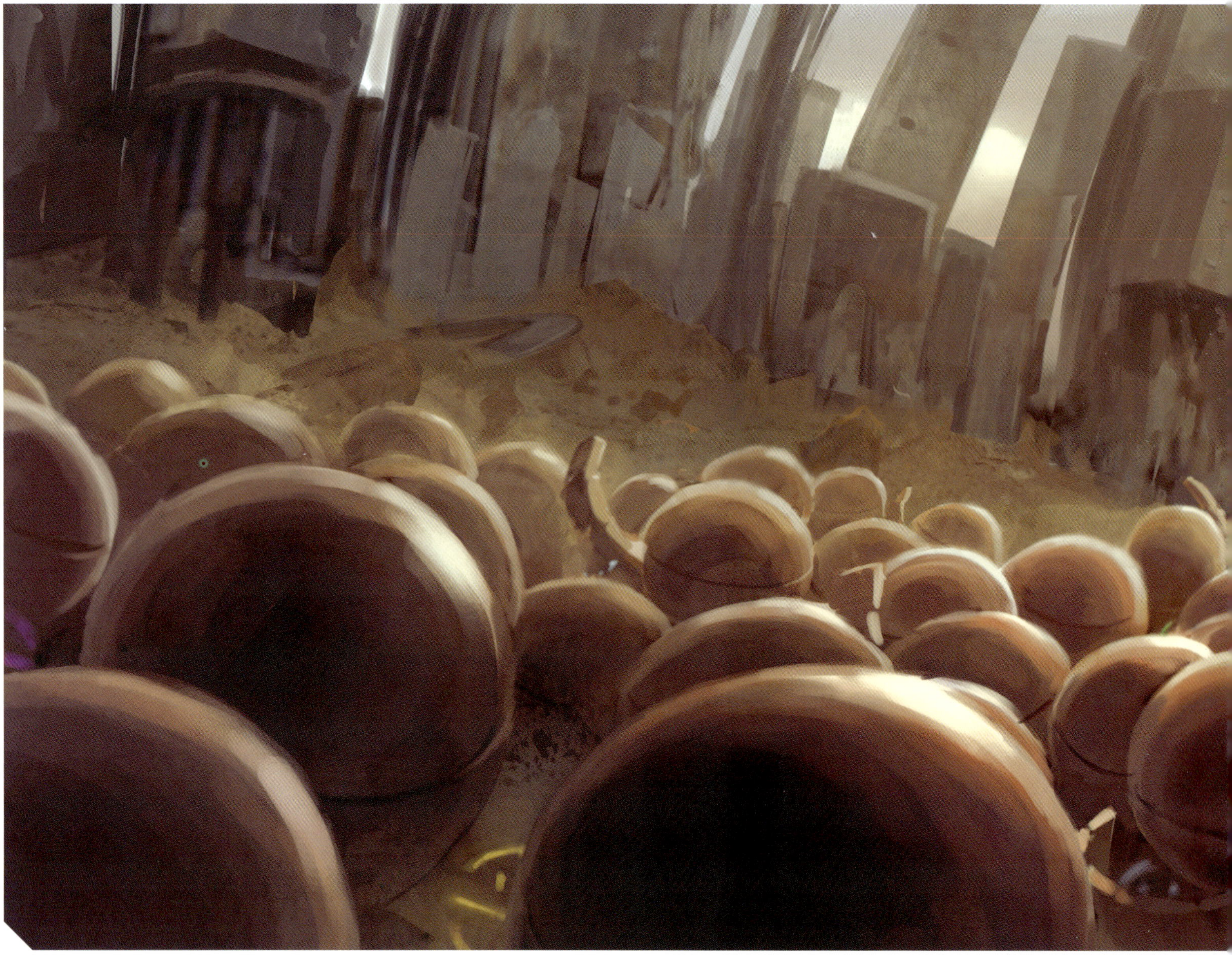

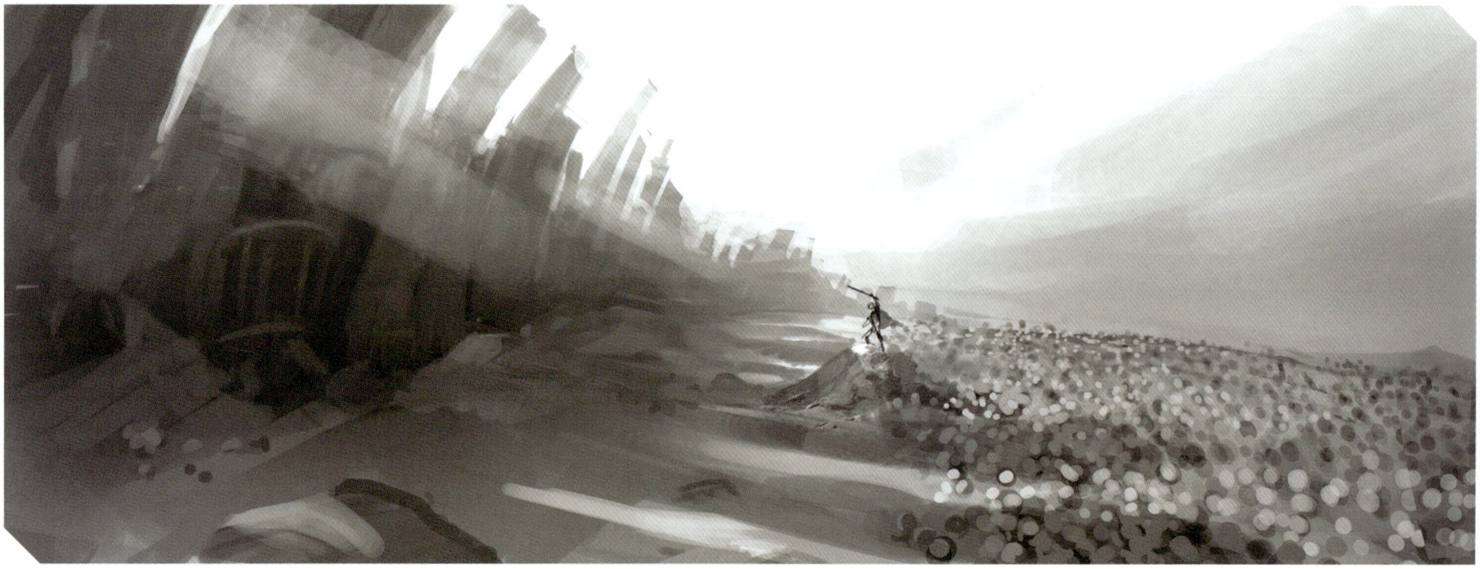

In a scene that proved too ambitious for the game, Joule leads an army of frames similar to Violet in a direct assault on Victor's fortress.

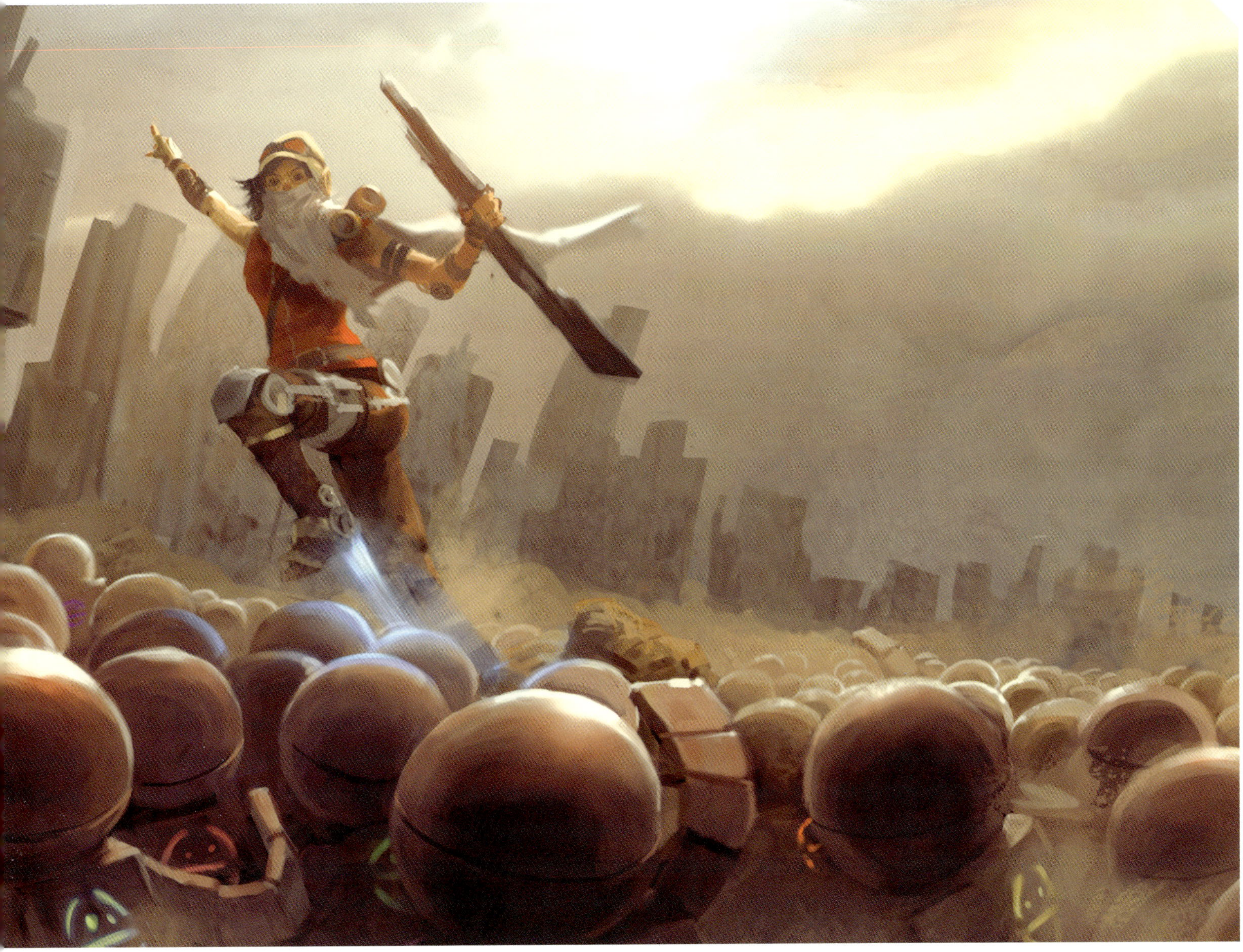

Craig Sellars

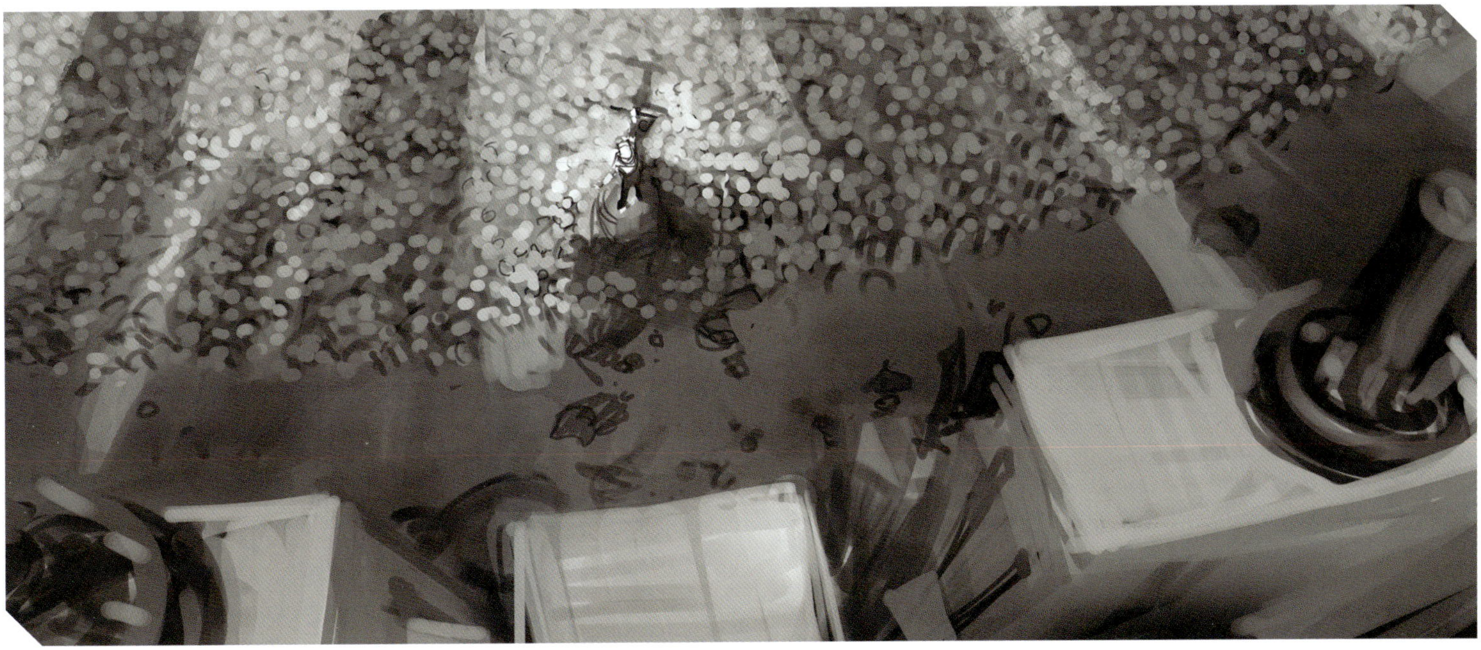

Craig Sellars

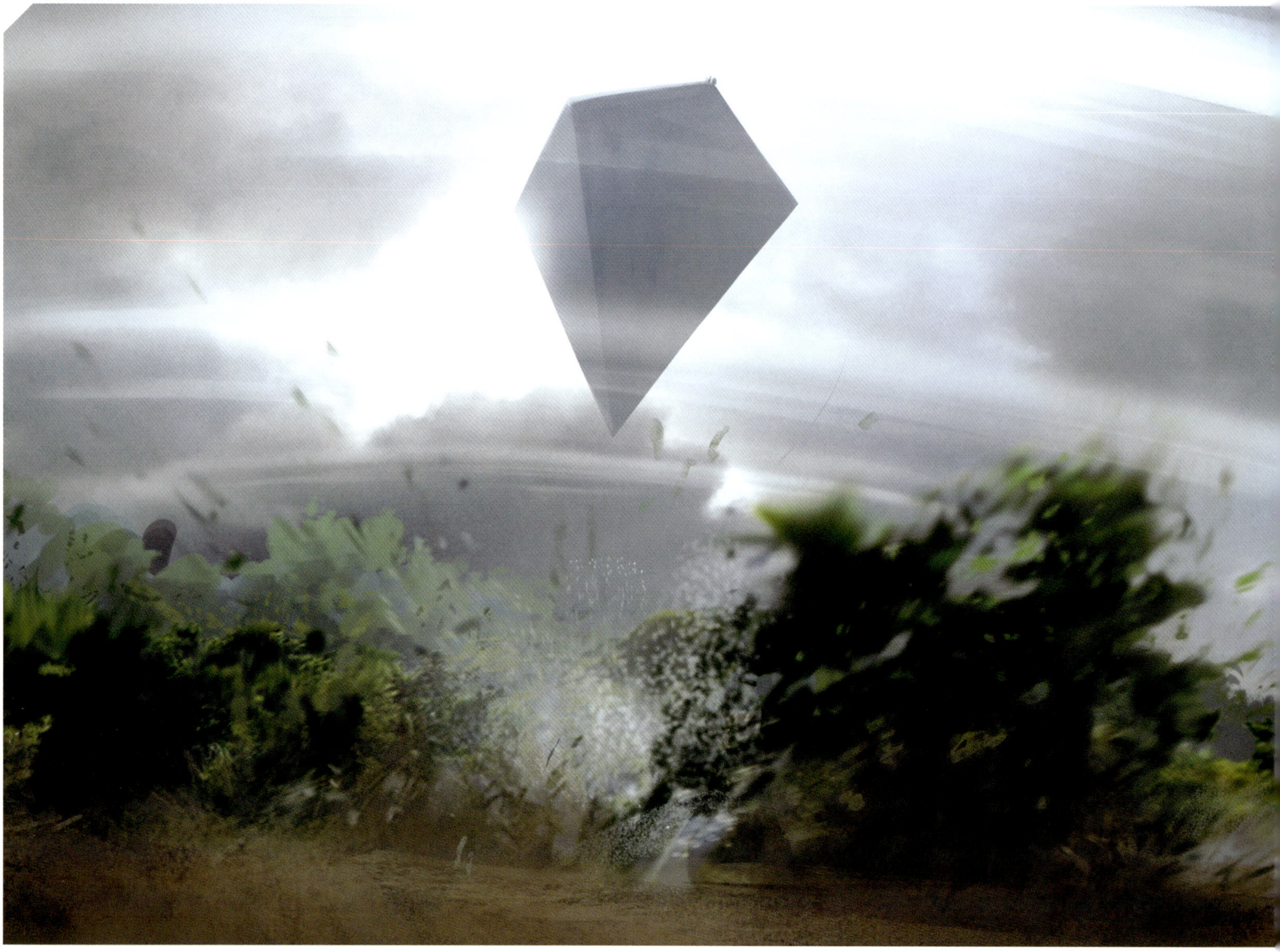

Craig Sellars

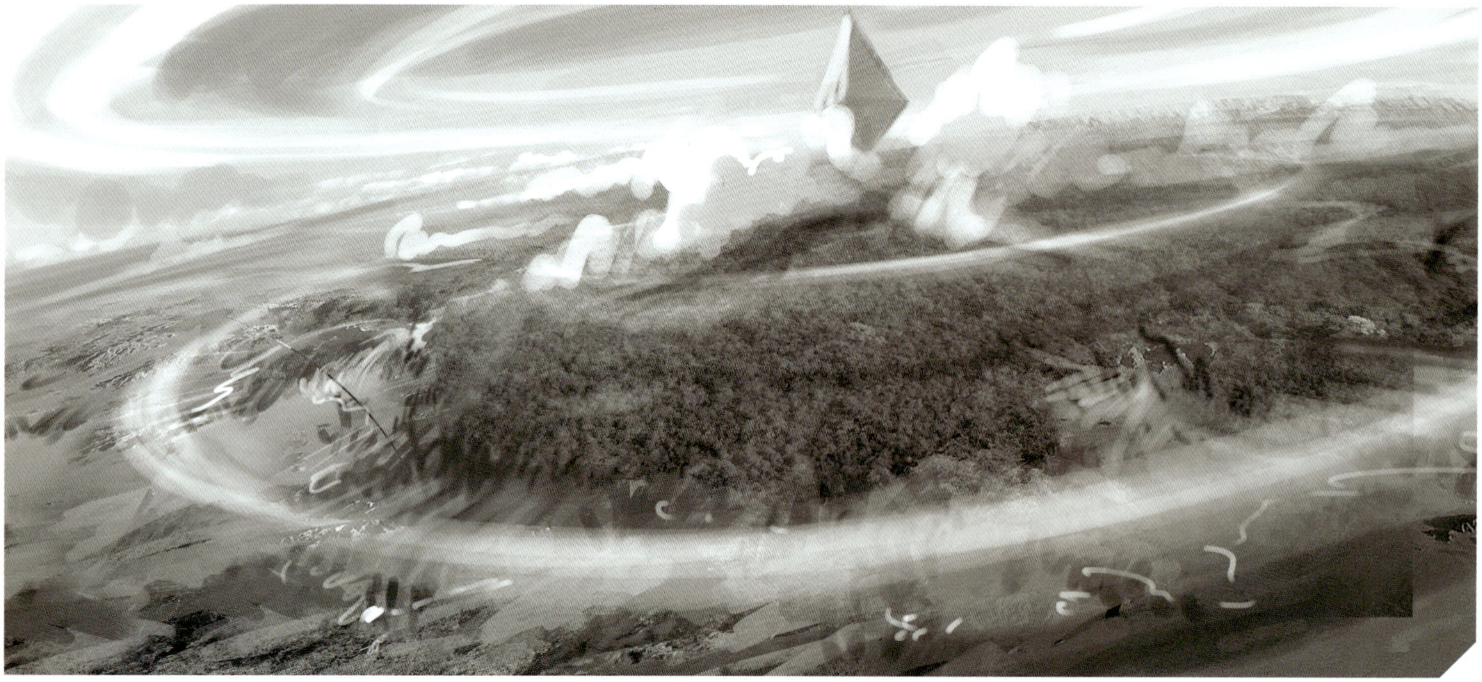

Hovic Alahaidoyan

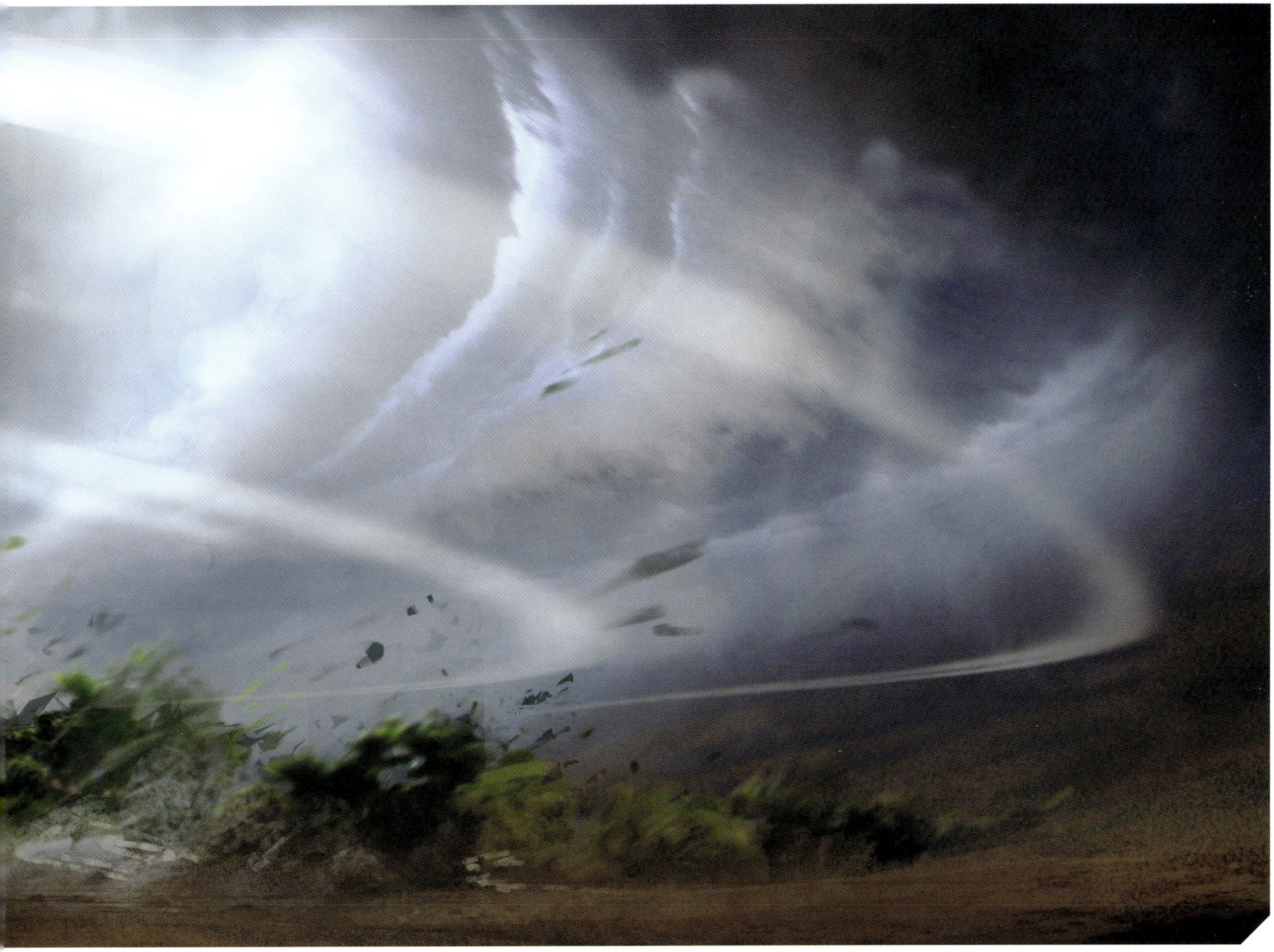

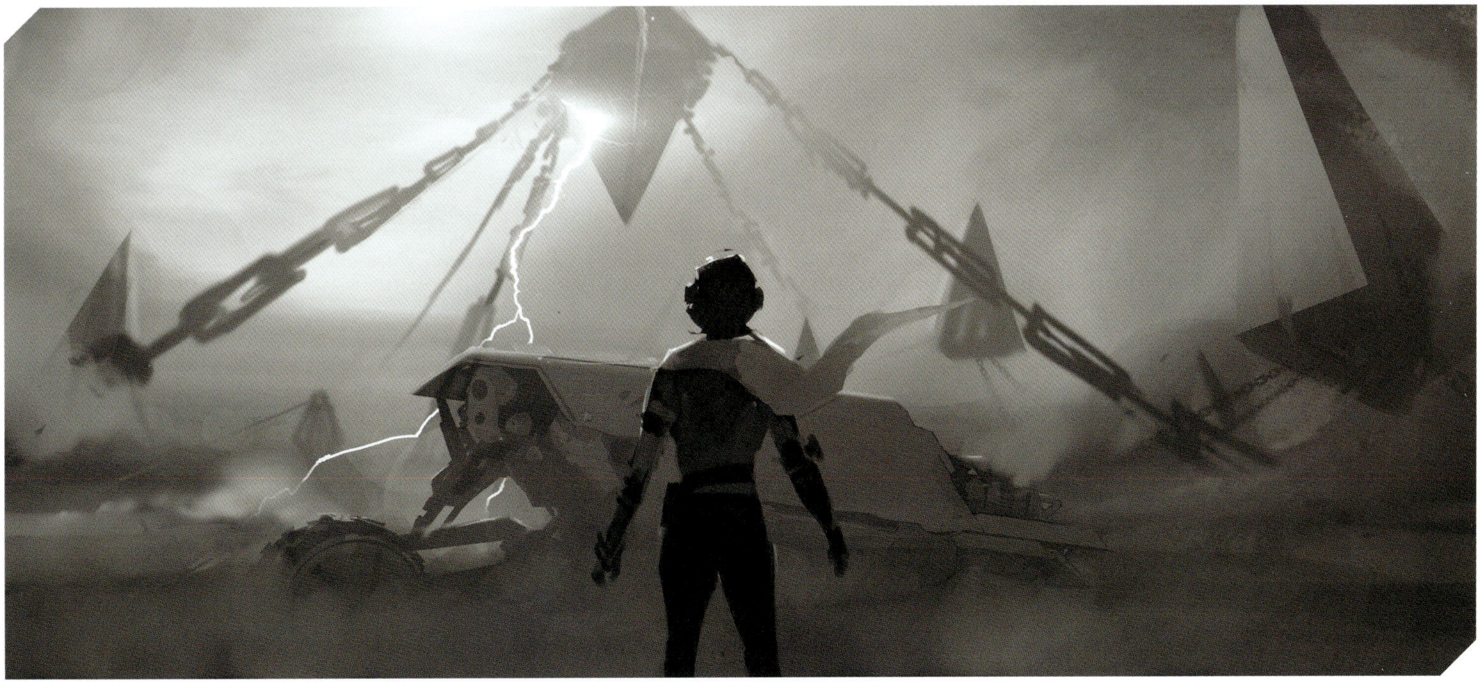

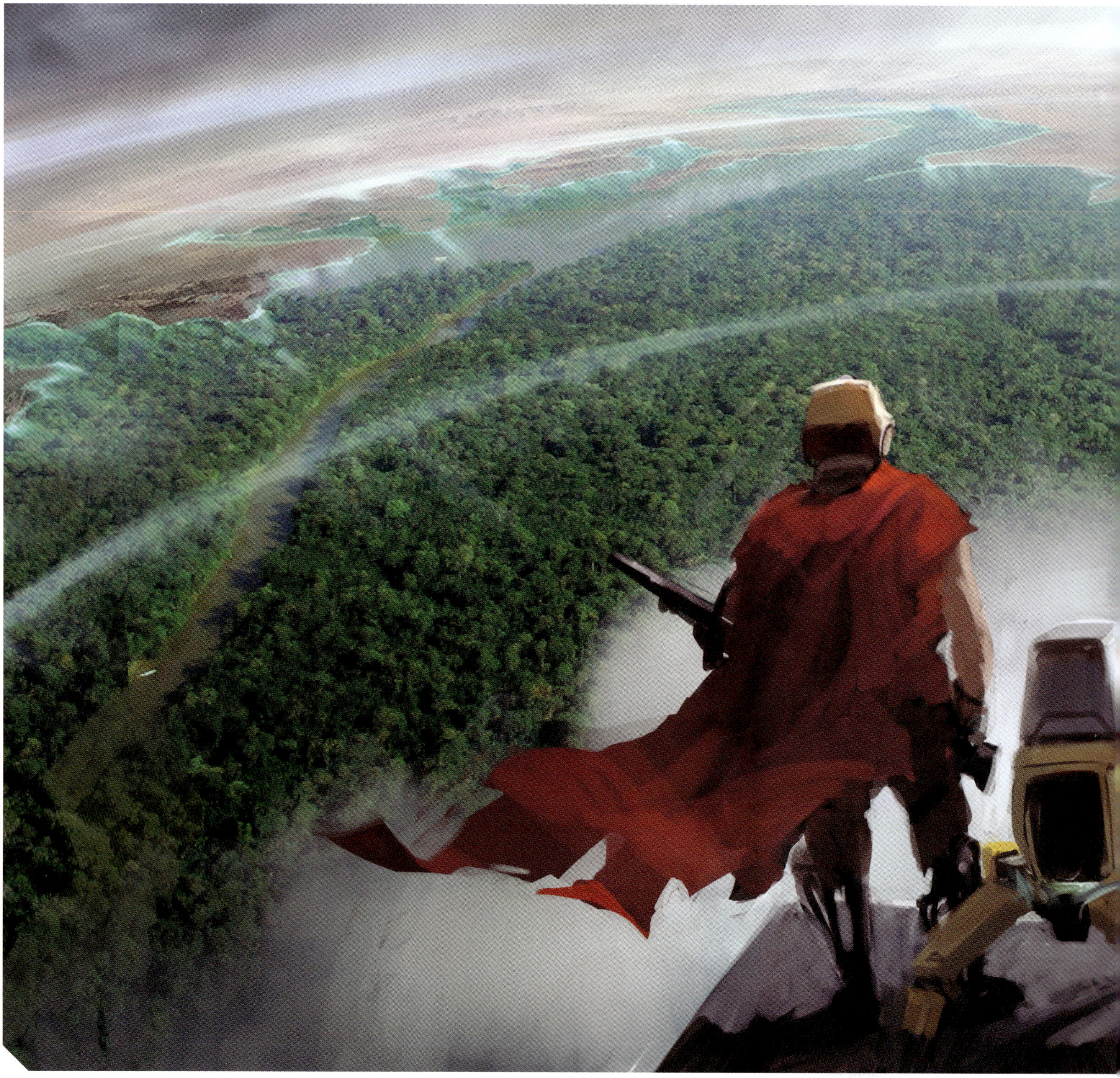

Another mood board captures Joule and Kai triumphantly standing atop Eden Tower and watching the terraforming system spring back to life.

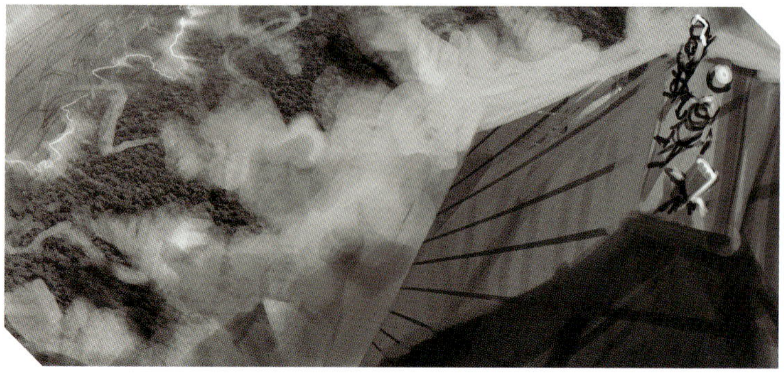

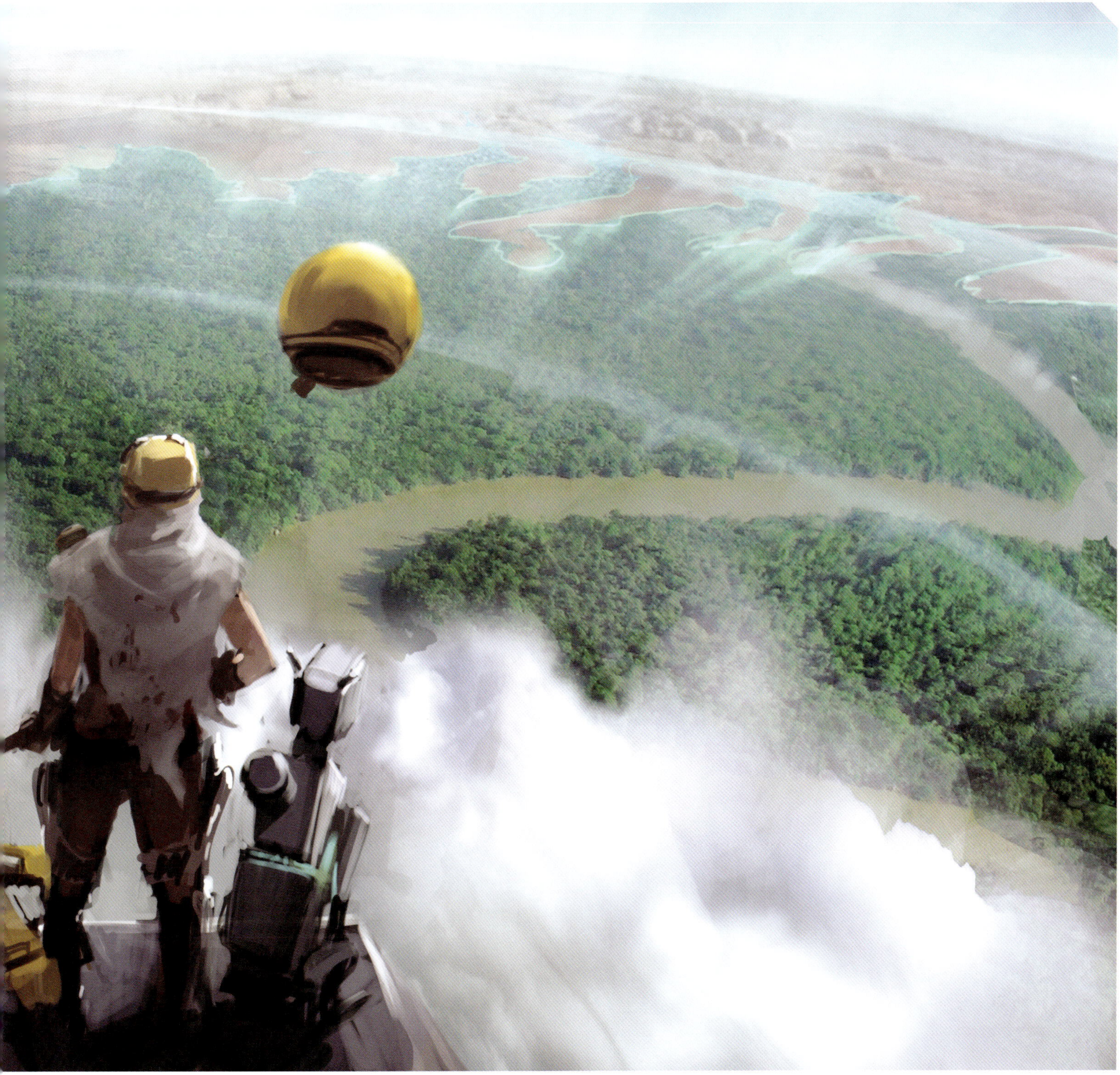

Craig Sellars

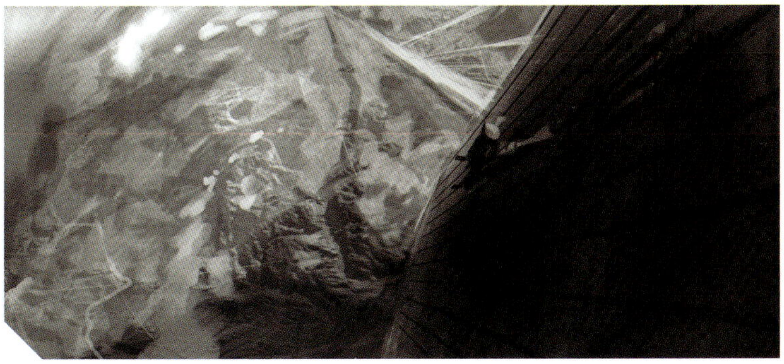

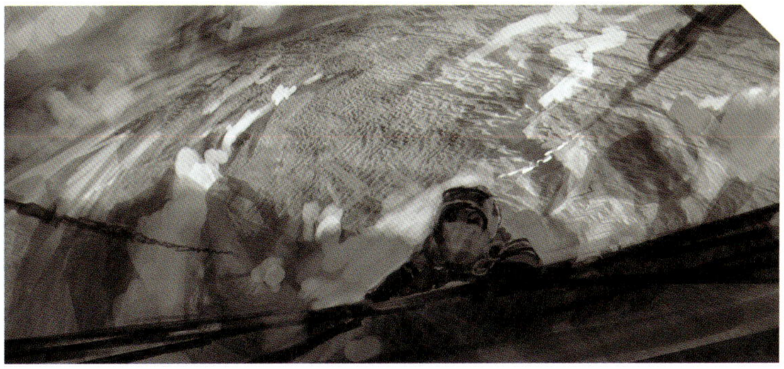

Craig Sellars

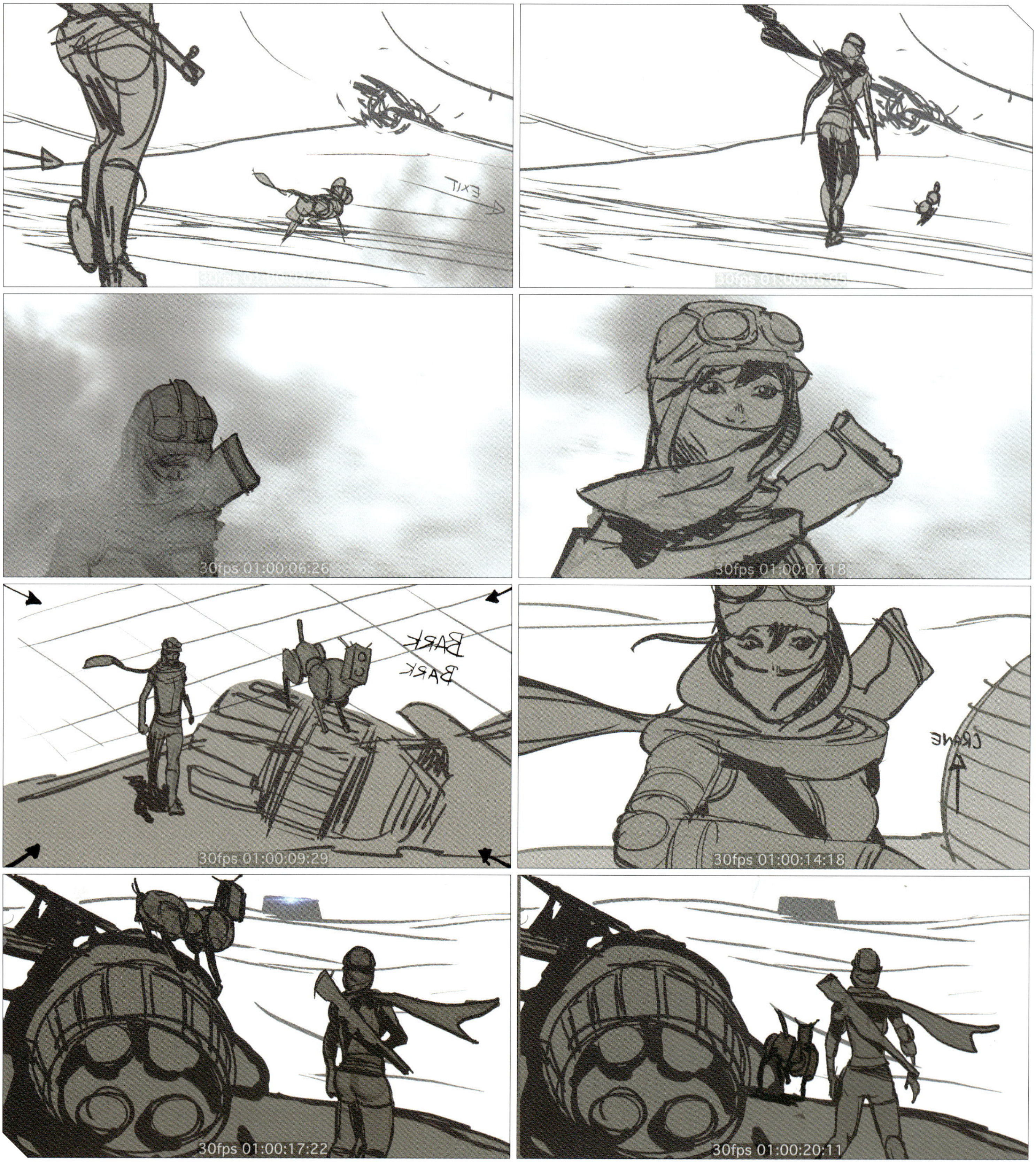
30fps 01:00:06:26
30fps 01:00:07:18
30fps 01:00:09:29
30fps 01:00:14:18
30fps 01:00:17:22
30fps 01:00:20:11

Chad Smith

Production storyboards and renders for the game's opening cinematic. These shots introduce Joule and Mack, on the hunt for a mysterious power source.

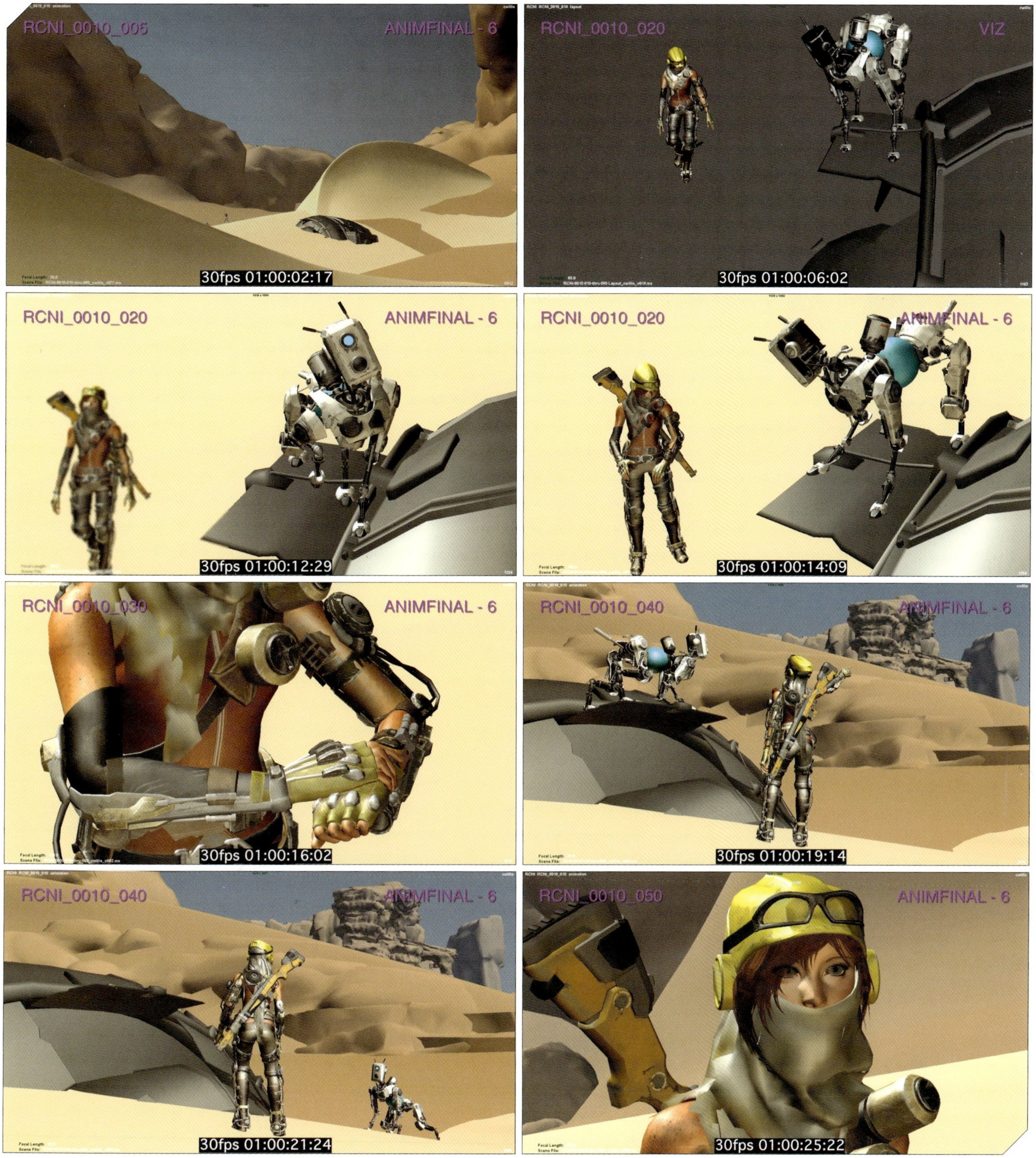
RCNI_0010_005
ANIMFINAL - 6
30fps 01:00:02:17
RCNI_0010_020
VIZ
30fps 01:00:06:02
RCNI_0010_020
ANIMFINAL - 6
30fps 01:00:12:29
RCNI_0010_020
ANIMFINAL - 6
30fps 01:00:14:09
RCNI_0010_030
ANIMFINAL - 6
30fps 01:00:16:02
RCNI_0010_040
ANIMFINAL - 6
30fps 01:00:19:14
RCNI_0010_040
ANIMFINAL - 6
30fps 01:00:21:24
RCNI_0010_050
ANIMFINAL - 6
30fps 01:00:25:22

Curtis Willis

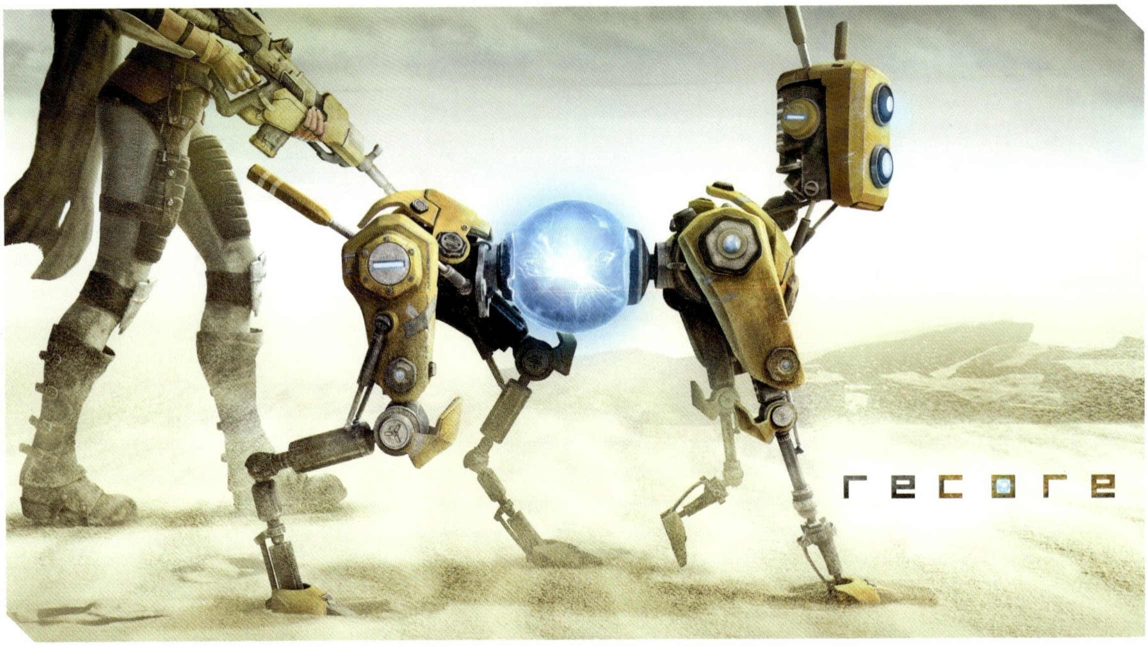
recore

Thank you to the contributing artists,
without whom this book wouldn't have been possible:

Armature

Alexis Boyer, Calum Watt, Capen Apple, Chris Percle, Dan Doherty, David Wright, Elizabeth Foster, Fannie Gunton, James Melsha, Jamie Clark, Jared Rudiak, Jason Marcil, Jason Owen, Justin Freeden, Kip Carbone, Kristoff Johnson, Manuel Zapata, Markel Milanes, Mary Monkowski, Nikita Carbone, Oliver Plunkett, Patrick Sullivan, Peter Kachtik, R. C. Torres, Scott Eaton, Scott Green, Todd Keller

Comcept

Daiki Kasubuchi, Shinsuke Komaki

Asobo

David Dedeine, Patrice Bourroncle, Julien Guérin, Andreas Nick, Fabrice Chaland, Emmanuel Lecouturierm, Loic Paulus, Antoine Lysson, Damien Papet, Olivier Cannone, Vincent Cazals, Thomas Chevenne, Kevin Dartoy, Franck Manon, Marco Puricelli, Pierre Lemasson, Xavier Courouau, Silvain Fernandes, Raghava Krishna Vadakkancheri Ravi, Thierry Puginier

Microsoft

Don Smith, Greg Bahm, Habib Zargarpour, Mike Spalding, Patrick Shettlesworth, Royal Winchester, Steve Hoogendyk

Gold Tooth

Armando Singh, Byron Lamarque, Chad Smith, Curtis Richardson-Smith, Curtis Willis, Dita Lang, Frank Benton, Garnet Fellhauer, Gian Inocencio, Giovanni Gasparetto, Hao Wang, Irene Pu, Jeff Wong, John Bresky, Kody Sabourin, Lianna Scrimger, Marc Stephenson, Mark Relf, Mike Ferraro, Nigel Rankin, Paul Furminger, Peter Saumur, Scott Paquin, Sean Horne, Simon Furminger, Skye White, Tyson Braddock

and

Artcore, Atomhawk, Craig Sellars, Etienne Jabbour, Hovic Alahaidoyan, Joe Bird, Marcel van Vuuren, Paul Richards, Ryan Denning, Sarma Vanguri, Thomas Pringle, Tom Rhodes, Wesley Burt

A very special thanks to our families for helping us bring this game to life.